BASIC INTERVIEWING SKILLS

014

BASIC INTERVIEWING SKILLS

A WORKBOOK FOR PRACTITIONERS

Valerie Nash Chang

Indiana University

with the assistance of

Sheryn T. Scott

Azusa Pacific University

Copyright © 1999 by Nelson-Hall Inc.
ISBN 0-8304-1530-0

Manufactured in the United States of America

Nelson-Hall Publishers / *Chicago*

Project Editor: Steven M. Long
Manufacturer: Capital City Press
Cover Painting: "Span-Red," by Anna Johnson

Copyright © 1999 by Nelson-Hall Inc.
ISBN 0-8304-1530-0

Manufactured in the United States of America

10 9 8 7 6 5 4 3 2

CONTENTS

Forward vii

I. Understanding the System 1

Role of Peer Supervisor 3

II. Basic Interpersonal Skills 5

Skill-Building 1: Communicating Involvement 7

Communicating Involvement Evaluation Form 9

Skill-Building 2: Observing 10

Observing Evaluation Form 13

Skill-Building 3: Active Listening 15

Active Listening Evaluation Form 18

Skill-Building 4: Beginning Behavior 20

Beginning Behavior Evaluation Form 23

III. Exploring Process 25

Written Exercise A: Identifying Feeling and
Content Statements 27

Written Exercise B: Writing Feeling and Content Statements . . 28

Inappropriate Responses 30

Skill-Building 5: Reflecting 32

Reflecting Evaluation Form 35

Skill-Building 6: Questioning 38

Questioning Evaluation Form 41

Skill-Building 7: Seeking Clarification 45

Seeking Clarification Evaluation Form 48

Written Exercise C: Advanced Reflecting Skills 53

Skill-Building 8: Advanced Reflecting 54

Advanced Reflecting Evaluation Form 57

Communication Scale 62

Written Exercise D: Naming Statements Using
the Communication Scale 64

IV.   Contracting Process 66

General Form of Responses from Reflecting through Reaching
Agreement about Goals 67

Complete Communication Scale 68

Examples of Contracting Responses 69

Example: Naming a Series of Transactions 69

Example: Personal Problems and Challenges 71

Written Exercise E: Recognizing Responses that Reach
Agreement about Problems and Challenges 73

Skill-Building 9: Reaching Agreement about Problems and
Challenges 74

Agreement about Problems Evaluation Form 76

Written Exercise F: Recognizing Responses that Reach
Agreement about Goals 80

Written Exercise G: Naming Responses Using
the Communication Scale 81

Skill-Building 10: Reaching Agreement about Goals 89

Agreement about Goals Evaluation Form 91

Written Exercise H: Creating Measurable, Attainable,
Positive, and Specific (MAPS) Goals 95

Skill-Building 11: Defining Goals and Establishing a Contract   96

Defining Goals and Establishing a Contract Evaluation Form . . 98

V. Evaluating Skills 102

Determining the Effectiveness of Your Responses 102

Process for Evaluating Videotapes 105

Final Videotape Evaluation Form 108

Appendix A: Description of Evaluation Scales 112

References 117

Index 119

FOREWORD

The system of learning described in this book began in my classes as I looked for ways to help my students master practice skills. Over the years, my students have made many contributions to this system. Their ideas about how to help them learn are integrated throughout the book. Their excitement and support for the value of this system been critical in my decision to continue to use, refine, and develop the system.

Moving the system from something I used to a book was always a dream but did not begin to gain momentum until my friend and colleague, Sheryn T. Scott, mentioned her frustration in helping her students master basic practice skills. I told her about the system I had developed and said that she was welcome to use it. In the last several years, Sheryn has been using this system herself and has taught it to other instructors. As she worked with the system, she pointed out areas that needed explanation, clarification, or description. With our joint efforts, the system has been greatly improved.

Several other people have been very helpful in this process. Another colleague who used this system is Grafton H. Hull. He liked it, thought it made a unique contribution, and encouraged me to talk with his publisher. Along the way Grafton has been consistently willing to offer suggestions. Christine Paseirbowicz, a student of mine, reviewed the most recent changes in the workbook and made many excellent suggestions. My dear friend, Stan Stackhouse offered support and suggestions throughout the process. Kathleen Kusta, President, Richard Meade, General Manager, Stephen Ferrara, and Steven Long, Associate Editor, at Nelson-Hall have been terrific to work with and very helpful at each step in the process.

UNDERSTANDING THE SYSTEM

You are about to begin an exciting part of your training to become a competent self-reflective professional. Competent practitioners are practitioners who have the knowledge and skills needed to perform their tasks (Hughes & Rycus, 1989). Competent practitioners engage in a continuous process of self-assessment and self-evaluation. They define goals related to professional development and identify their strengths and areas for growth related to skill development and knowledge acquisition (Bernotavicz, 1994). The goal of competency-based education is for students to have solid theoretical knowledge and the ability to use that knowledge and related skills effectively in their work with clients. Competent beginning professionals have practiced basic skills to the point that "they are no longer conscious of applying them" (Weick, 1993, p. 28), can focus on true dialogue and contact with their clients, and can acquire an understanding of their clients' reality (Mahoney, 1986; Vodde & Gallant, 1995).

While using this book, you will focus on one group of skills at a time. You will learn how to appropriately use the skills and to evaluate your use of the skills. With each practice session your use of the skills will improve. Eventually, you will be able to use these skills automatically with the same degree of ease as driving a car or using a computer.

Using the workbook, you will learn the following important basic practice skills:

- to establish an appropriate beginning structure and communicate involvement with a client;
- to actively listen, fully observe, and hear the client;
- to use appropriate and accurate reflection of feeling, content, and/or meaning as well as to summarize client statements;
- to appropriately use open-ended and close-ended questions;
- to explore the basic information about the person(s), the challenge(s), and the situation;
- to adequately seek clarification;
- to reflect pertinent themes that go beyond what the client has articulated;

1

- to identify the problems or challenges for work;
- to set goals with clients;
- to define goals so that they are measurable, attainable, positive, and specific;
- to establish ways to evaluate goal achievement and create a basic plan for work;
- to appropriately express warmth, respect, empathy, and genuineness to clients; and
- to constructively evaluate your work and give constructive feedback to others.

After developing an adequate repertoire of basic interviewing skills, you can move on to more advanced skills, can develop a personal style or way to more fully include yourself in the process, can learn to use skills effectively with a wide variety of clients in many different situations, and can learn to put all your skills together in a therapeutic manner. As these basic skills become automatic, you will be able to focus more completely on the process with your clients. Your ability to be empathic, warm, respectful, and genuine will increase as your confidence in the use of the basic skills increases. Ultimately, the goal is for you to become an effective, reflective practitioner who uses self-evaluation, learns from mistakes and successes, and is continuously improving.

As was mentioned earlier, you will learn skills by focusing on one skill group at a time. After mastering one group of skills, you will move on to the next discrete group of skills, with each new group of skills building on the previously practiced skills.

You will be using several methods of learning related to each skill.

Reading You will read about the use of the skill in this workbook and probably in other books. Your instructor will discuss the use of the skill and may invite you to talk about your ideas concerning the use of this skill.

Writing With some of the skills, you will have written exercises to complete before moving on to actual practice.

Discussing Before actually doing each practice exercise, you will have an opportunity to review the directions and ask questions about the practice exercise and the use of the skill. With the more advanced skills, you may have an opportunity to see the skill in use either with a role-play or a videotaped vignette.

Visualizing As you read through the directions for the exercises, make a mental image of

yourself using the skill and pay attention to any questions you have about the correct use of the skill.

Doing   Now you are ready to actually practice using the skills. You will work with two other students. Each of you will have a chance to be in the role of client, practitioner, and peer supervisor.

Evaluating   Immediate feedback is a central part of this system. After each practice session, the person in the role of the client will give feedback focusing on whether he/she felt understood and thought there was an honest connection with the practitioner, the practitioner will identify what she/he thinks were strengths and weaknesses, and the peer supervisor will give the practitioner feedback on the use of skills. To facilitate this process, the peer supervisor will complete an evaluation form.

Role of Peer Supervisor

Your role as peer supervisor is very important. There is no way that your instructor can watch each student. Even if that were possible, it would not give you the chance to develop your skills as a supervisor. Throughout your career you will be evaluating your own work and many of you will eventually be supervising others. Although the many jobs of the peer supervisor are challenging to learn, your peer supervisor skills will have almost as many benefits as learning the practitioner skills. You may think that since you are a beginner, you can't give constructive, useful feedback. In fact, by carefully following the directions in this workbook, you can give very helpful feedback and can learn to effectively supervise yourself and others.

1.   *Give constructive and accurate feedback*   You are the mirror reflecting back to the practitioner both his or her strengths and areas for growth. It may seem like you should say only positive things to the practitioners, but this would not be an accurate reflection and would not help them improve their skills. Before giving feedback think

about the kind of feedback you would find helpful. Would it help you if the peer supervisor chose not to tell you about some problem and let you continue doing the same thing incorrectly? Your goal as peer supervisor is to help the practitioner improve. Remember that each person in this class wants to learn these skills.

2. *Give specific feedback.* It is not helpful to say you did a fine job. Tell the person specifically what she/he did that you saw as positive or negative and, if possible, tell her/him what impact you think her/his behavior might have had on the client. For example, you might say, "You leaned toward your client and looked directly at her. After you did that for a while I noticed your client seemed to relax." Or, "You frequently fidgeted with your pencil. I noticed your client looking at the pencil. I think your behavior might have been distracting to your client."

3. *Focus on the behavior not on the person.* For example, say, "You leaned back in your chair." Rather than "You didn't pay attention to your client."

4. *Complete the evaluation form.* Record feedback that the practitioner received from you and the client. Use the evaluation form in the practitioner's book so the practitioner will have a record of how he/she did. At the completion of each exercise, you may be asked to turn the evaluation sheet in for your instructor to review.

II

BASIC INTERPERSONAL SKILLS

Use of basic interpersonal skills is essential for effective relationships with individuals, families, groups, communities, or organizations. These skills communicate that the practitioner is fully present. The purpose of this first group of skills is to involve the client in the process.

In this section, you will focus on the following skills: Communicating Involvement, Observing, Active Listening, and Beginning Process skills. Each of these skills are activities that most of us tend to believe we can automatically do well. They seem like behaviors used in every day life. Actually, we rarely pay attention to the messages our physical posture may be sending to another person, often do not closely observe the other person, seldom focus fully on another person, and usually hear without listening. These basic interpersonal behaviors are crucial elements of a positive relationship with your clients. Good relationships rest on effectively communicating involvement, accurately observing, and actively listening.

After working on communicating involvement, accurately observing, and actively listening, you will learn to effectively begin your meetings with clients. The first few minutes of any meeting or relationship tends to set the tone. You know from your own experience how important first impressions can be and how much these first impressions may effect the future of the relationship. Now stop and think about a time when you had a meeting with a professional person who was new to you. I imagine you felt much more comfortable with those professionals who fully explained the process and told you what to expect. Remember that when you begin with clients.

Beginning behavior skills are essential to creating an atmosphere conducive to productive work together. Clients are generally anxious and do not know what to expect. It is up to you to explain the process to them. In these critical first few minutes, the practitioner can allay some of the client's anxiety by explaining the ground rules for meeting, by inviting the client to introduce him- or herself and tell you how he or she wants to be addressed, by stating the purpose of the meeting, and by asking the client if he/she has any questions. In many situations, it will also be important to explain relevant agency policies and

any ethical factors that you are required to clarify such as a signed consent for treatment, limits of confidentiality, fees and method of acceptable payment, and the type of license under which you are working.

Skill-Building 1: Communicating Involvement

Objective of Exercise: To practice the behaviors that communicate your readiness to listen, your interest in your client, your willingness to work with your client, your attentiveness, and your general involvement with the process. These behaviors say to your client, "I am here and I am ready and willing to be with you now."

Behaviors that Communicate Involvement:

1. Open and accessible body posture: This says, "I am open to you. I am not feeling defensive."

2. Congruent facial expressions: Your expressions should express your feelings. If the client is talking about something sad and/or serious, you will probably be feeling concerned or serious and your face should reflect this feeling experience.

3. Slightly inclined toward the client: This tends to say to your client that you are attentive.

4. Directly face the client with about four feet of distance between you: This is generally a comfortable distance that does not intrude upon the other person's space.

5. Regular eye contact unless inappropriate because of cultural customs: You do not want to stare at your clients, but you should generally maintain eye contact with them as a way to show your interest in them.

6. Eliminate distracting behaviors: Any type of distracting behavior draws attention to itself and away from the process. So if you tend to play with your fingers, twiddle with your pencil, fidget, rock in your chair, swing your legs, wind your hair on your finger, and so on, you will need to remind yourself to stop these behaviors.

7. Use minimal encouragement: Doing such things as nodding your head and saying "huh, huh" tends to let you clients know your are paying attention to them. Repeating one of the last words in your client's sentence is another way to offer minimal encouragement. For example, if your client said, "I am worried about what my supervisor will say." You could say, "your supervisor?" letting your client know you heard them and inviting them to continue.

Directions for the Exercise:

1. Form groups of three people. You will each be in the roles of the practitioner, peer supervisor, and client.

2. The practitioner will begin by mentally reviewing the behaviors that communicate involvement. During the interview, the practitioner will use all the behaviors that indicate involvement. The practitioner will listen, staying silent except for using sounds or words that communicate minimal encouragement.

3. The client will tell a two-minute story.

4. After the client finishes, the client will share how he/she experienced the practitioner, focusing on whether it felt like the practitioner was fully involved.

5. The practitioner will evaluate her/his use of the behaviors that communicate involvement.

6. The peer supervisor will evaluate the practitioner's use of behaviors that communicate involvement and fill out the evaluation form. (Use the practitioner's book so that person will have the feedback for future reference.) The peer supervisor will give one point for each behavior used by the practitioner.

7. The peer supervisor will then evaluate how well the practitioner communicated involvement using the evaluation scale.

Communicating Involvement Evaluation Scale

Level 1: The practitioner communicates involvement very little of the time.
Level 2: The practitioner communicates involvement some of the time.
Level 3: The practitioner communicates involvement most of the time.
Level 4: The practitioner communicates involvement almost all the time.
Level 5: The practitioner communicates involvement all of the time.

Using this scale the peer supervisor will evaluate how much of the time the practitioner was using the behaviors that communicate involvement. Remember as peer supervisor, giving your most honest evaluation will be most helpful. Giving the person a high score just to be nice will not help the person know what he/she needs to work on. Circle the number that best describes your evaluation. Write the total score on the evaluation form.

8. Continue until each person has been in each role.

Communicating Involvement Evaluation Form

Name of Practitioner_____

Name of Peer Supervisor_____

Directions: Under each category (in italics) is a list of behaviors or skills. Give one point for each specific behavior or skill exhibited by the practitioner. On the scales, circle the number that best represents your evaluation of the appropriateness, effectiveness, or completeness of the practitioner's overall use of the skills or behaviors in the category.

Basic Interpersonal Skills

Communicating Involvement: Give one point for each behavior used by the practitioner. Using the scale, circle the number that represents your evaluation of the effectiveness of the practitioner's overall use of behaviors that communicate involvement.

1.	Open and accessible body posture	_____
2.	Congruent facial expression	_____
3.	Slightly inclined toward the client	_____
4.	Directly face the client	_____
4.	Regular eye contact unless inappropriate	_____
5.	No distracting behavior	_____
6.	Minimal encouragement	_____

Communicating Involvement Evaluation Scale

Level 1:   The practitioner communicates involvement very little of the time.
Level 2:   The practitioner communicates involvement some of the time.
Level 3:   The practitioner communicates involvement most of the time.
Level 4:   The practitioner communicates involvement almost all the time.
Level 5:   The practitioner communicates involvement all of the time.

1	2	3	4	5	_____
Ineffective				Highly Effective	Score

Total Score: Add each point and the circled number to get the total score for the interview.

_____
Score

Skill-Building 2: Observing

Objective of Exercise: Some people are naturally excellent observers while others tend to focus on what is being said and forget to pay attention to other modes of communication. The purpose of this exercise is too heighten your awareness of nonverbal communication. Observations of you client's facial expressions, eye movement and eye contact, body position and general movement, breathing patterns, muscle tone, gestures, and skin tone changes will help you notice possible incongruity between verbal and nonverbal content and will help you understand the intensity of your client's feelings, general energy level, and relationship with you (Carkhuff & Anthony, 1979). For example, if your client sat slumped in his chair, leaning away from you, rarely moving, and looking mostly at the ceiling, what might you suspect about his energy level and relationship with you?

Careful observations supplement verbal input, sometimes intensifying what is being said and sometimes contradicting what is said. If your client became flushed when talking about a particular topic, you might guess that your client had strong feelings about that topic even if his/her words were not reporting strong feelings.

Directions for Exercise:

1. Form groups of three people. You will each play the roles of the practitioner, client, and peer supervisor.

2. The client will think of an experience in which he/she had a strong feeling reaction. Silently remember this scene, visualizing it as fully as possible. Let your body show how you felt. Take a couple of minutes to complete this task. You will not be asked to discuss this scene.

3. After mentally reviewing behavior that communicates involvement and thinking about the importance of observation, the practitioner will use the behaviors that communicate involvement and observe the client. The practitioner will be silent except for the use of minimal encouragement.

4. During the interview, the peer supervisor will watch the practitioner's use of behaviors that communicate involvement and will observe the client.

The following activities will be completed after the interview:

5. The client will share how he/she experienced the practitioner.

6. The practitioner will evaluate her/his use of observation skills.

7. The peer supervisor will check the practitioner's use of the behaviors that

communicate involvement and will evaluate the practitioner's use of communicating involvement.

8.   The peer supervisor will ask the practitioner about observations related to each of the seven points on the evaluation form. The peer supervisor will ask for description rather than evaluations. For example, "the client looked down, had tears in her eyes, her mouth was turned down, and she sat slumped with little movement" rather than "she seemed depressed." As peer supervisor, listen for descriptions of facial expressions that include brow, corners of eyes, mouth, nostrils, pupils. On eye movement, the practitioner will describe whether the client's eyes looked up, down, across and whether the client maintained eye contact or did not. When discussing body posture, the practitioner will describe how the client was sitting, and whether the client was rigid, relaxed, slouched. Related to movement, the practitioner will describe head, arm and leg movement. Breathing patterns are usually regular but sometimes slow down, speed up, or involve sighs. Muscle tone can be described as rigid, tense, relaxed. Gestures can be described by quantity (none, some, a great deal) and type (made a fist and pounded on the desk, moved hands in a circle, rotated arms so palms faced up and them down). The practitioner will note changes such as "began by sitting rigidly and became relaxed." Remember to use the evaluation form in the practitioner's book.

9.   Using the evaluation scale, the peer supervisor will evaluate how well the practitioner was able to describe what he/she observed.

Observing Evaluation Scale

Level 1:   The practitioner is not able to describe any aspects of the client's behavior. Level 2:The practitioner's descriptions are minimal.

Level 3:   The practitioner is able to give some description of each of the seven aspects of the client's behavior.

Level 4:   The practitioner is able to give adequate descriptions of each of the seven aspects of the client's behavior.

Level 5:   The practitioner is able to give full and complete descriptions of each of the seven aspects of the client's behavior.

Using the scale, the peer supervisor will evaluate the completeness of the practitioner's description. For example, one practitioner might say in describing facial expression, "The client smiled a lot." This might be accurate but is less fully developed than the following description. Another practitioner might say, "In the beginning of the meeting the client smiled and went back to smiling most of the time. However, she frowned when

talking about her son and got a bit teary when talking about her mother." The second description includes the level of detail that could be part of a description that would receive a score of 5.

10. The practitioner guesses what feelings the client was experiencing.

11. The client states what he/she was feeling.

12. Continue until each person has been in each role.

Observing Evaluation Form

Name of Practitioner_____

Name of Peer Supervisor_____

Directions: Under each category (in italics) is a list of behaviors or skills. Give one point for each specific behavior or skill exhibited by the practitioner. On the scales, circle the number that best represents your evaluation of the appropriateness, effectiveness, or completeness of the practitioner's overall use of the skills or behaviors in the category.

Basic Interpersonal Skills

Communicating Involvement: Give one point for each behavior used by the practitioner. Using the scale, circle the number that represents your evaluation of the effectiveness of the practitioner's overall use of behaviors that communicate involvement.

1.	Open and accessible body posture	_____
2.	Congruent facial expression	_____
3.	Slightly inclined toward the client	_____
4.	Directly face the client	_____
4.	Regular eye contact unless inappropriate	_____
5.	No distracting behavior	_____
6.	Minimal encouragement	_____

1	2	3	4	5
Ineffective				Highly Effective

Observing: The practitioner will describe the client. Give one point for each item described accurately. Using the scale, circle the number that best represents your evaluation of the overall completeness of the practitioner's descriptions.

1.	Facial expression	_____
2.	Eye movement and contact	_____
3.	Body position and movement	_____
4.	Breathing patterns	_____
5.	Muscle tone	_____
6.	Gestures	_____
7.	Skin tone changes	_____

Observing Evaluation Scale

Level 1:   The practitioner is not able to describe any aspects of the client's behavior.

Level 2:   The practitioner's descriptions are minimal.

Level 3:   The practitioner is able to give some description of each of the seven aspects of the client's behavior.

Level 4:   The practitioner is able to give adequate descriptions of each of the seven aspects of the client's behavior.

Level 5:   The practitioner is able to give full and complete descriptions of each of the seven aspects of the client's behavior.

1	2	3	4	5	
Incomplete				Complete	Score

Total Score: Add each point and each circled number to get the total score for the interview.

_____
Score

Skill-Building 3: Active Listening

Objective of Listening: To accurately understand the client's thoughts and feelings. Listening involves not only hearing the words, but making every effort to understand the meanings the other person is trying to convey and what the material means to the other person.

Objective of Exercise: To listen to what the client is expressing and to be able to accurately repeat what the client said.

Directions for Exercise:

1.   Form groups of three people. You will each take turns being the practitioner, client, and peer supervisor.

2.   The client will discuss any subject for five minutes. The client should do almost all of the talking.

3.   After mentally reviewing what he/she plans to do, the practitioner will communicate involvement, observe the client, and listen. Do not give any verbal responses beyond minimal encouragement.

4.   During the interview, the peer supervisor will watch the practitioner's use of behaviors that communicate involvement, observe the client, listen to the client, and keep track of time. The peer supervisor should do the evaluation in the practitioner's book so that person will have the feedback for future reference.

The following activities will be completed after the interview:

5.   The client will share how he/she experienced the practitioner.

6.   The practitioner will evaluate her/his use of listening skills.

7.   As in the previous exercise, the peer supervisor will evaluate the practitioner use of behaviors that communicate involvement, will ask the practitioner to describe what he/she observed in the client.

8.   The peer supervisor will ask the practitioner to repeat what he/she heard the client say and ask the practitioner to describe how the client spoke including speaking style, volume of speaking, and speed of delivery. The peer supervisor should ask the following kinds of questions:

a.   Did you notice any shifts in the conversation?

b.   Did you forget to listen at any time? If so, when? Do you have any ideas about why you stopped listening?

c.   Did anything happen that made it hard for you to listen?

d.   Did you hear any changes in the volume and speed of the client's speech?

e.   How would you describe the client's speaking style?

f.   How loud was the client's speech?

g.   How fast or slow did the client speak?

9.   The peer supervisor will evaluate the accuracy of the practitioner's summary of what the client said and description of the client's speaking style, volume of speaking, and speed of delivery. For example, the practitioner might say, "The client had a clear, direct, logical way of speaking. His volume was rather quiet, but he tended to talk louder when discussing his son. He spoke rather slowly and deliberately." If this description was accompanied by a good summary of what the client said, the practitioner could be given a score of 5.

10.   The peer supervisor will complete the evaluation scale related to active listening.

Active Listening: Content and Process Evaluation Scale

Level 1:   The practitioner is not able to give any of the major elements of content or describe the ways the client spoke.

Level 2:   The practitioner is able to minimally summarize some of the major elements of content and minimally able to describe the client's way of speaking.

Level 3:   The practitioner is able to moderately summarize and describe many of the major elements of content and moderately able to describe the clients way of speaking.

Level 4:   The practitioner is able to give a general summary describing most of the major elements of content and a general description of the client's way of speaking.

Level 5:   The practitioner is able to give a complete summary describing the major elements of content and accurately and fully describe the client's way of speaking including: speaking style, vocal tone and volume and speed of delivery.

Using this scale, you will evaluate how completely and accurately the practitioner

is able to describe the major elements of content and the client's way of speaking.

11.   Continue until each person has been in each role.

Active Listening Evaluation Form

Name of Practitioner_____

Name of Peer Supervisor_____

Directions: Under each category (in italics) is a list of behaviors or skills. Give one point for each specific behavior or skill exhibited by the practitioner. On the scales, circle the number that best represents your evaluation of the appropriateness, effectiveness, or completeness of the practitioner's overall use of the skills or behaviors in the category.

Basic Interpersonal Skills

Communicating Involvement: Give one point for each behavior used by the practitioner. Using the scale, circle the number that represents your evaluation of the effectiveness of the practitioner's overall use of behaviors that communicate involvement.

1.	Open and accessible body posture	_____
2.	Congruent facial expression	_____
3.	Slightly inclined toward the client	_____
4.	Directly face the client	_____
4.	Regular eye contact unless inappropriate	_____
5.	No distracting behavior	_____
6.	Minimal encouragement	_____

1   2   3   4   5

Ineffective   Highly Effective

Observing: The practitioner will describe the client. Give one point for each item described accurately. Using the scale, circle the number that best represents your evaluation of the overall completeness of the practitioner's descriptions.

1.	Facial expression	_____
2.	Eye movement and contact	_____
3.	Body position and movement	_____
4.	Breathing patterns	_____
5.	Muscle tone	_____
6.	Gestures	_____
7.	Skin tone changes	_____

1   2   3   4   5

Incomplete   Complete

Active Listening Skills—Content and Process: Using the scale, circle the number that best represents your evaluation of the accuracy and completeness of the practitioner's summary of what the client said and description of the client's way of speaking including speaking style,

vocal tone and volume, and speed of delivery.

<u>Active Listening: Content and Process Evaluation Scale</u>

Level 1:   The practitioner is not able to give any of the major elements of content or describe the ways the client spoke.

Level 2:   The practitioner is able to minimally summarize some of the major elements of content and minimally able to describe the client's way of speaking.

Level 3:   The practitioner is able to moderately summarize and describe many of the major elements of content and moderately able to describe the client's way of speaking.

Level 4:   The practitioner is able to give a general summary describing most of the major elements of content and a general description of the client's way of speaking.

Level 5:   The practitioner is able to give a complete summary describing the major elements of content and accurately and fully describe the client's way of speaking including: speaking style, vocal tone and volume, and speed of delivery.

1	2	3	4	5	
Inadequate				Complete	Score

Total Score Add each point and each circled number to get the total score for the interview.

_____
Score

Skill-Building 4: Beginning Behavior

Objective of Exercise: The purpose of this exercise is to practice making beginning statements. Every session needs to begin with some structure. The first session should include introductions, discussion of how each person prefers to be addressed, basic information such as where the meeting will take place, and how long the meeting will last. You also need to talk about the role of the practitioner including some information about what you will do, about your expectations of the client, and about your thoughts about the purpose of the meeting. In many cases, it is also important to talk about such things as agency policies and ethical guidelines. This part of the meeting should end by asking if your client has any questions.

Directions for Exercise:

1. Form groups of three people. You will each take turns being in the roles of the practitioner, client, and peer supervisor.

2. You will have an easier time doing well on this exercise if you write out and practice your beginning statement before class. Be sure to include the following information:
   a. state your first and last name;
   b. mention your profession, the name of your agency, and your role;
   c. ask how to pronounce client's name if you are not sure;
   d. ask how your client wants to be addressed, first names, titles, formal names, and so on;
   e. state where you will be meeting;
   f. identify how long the meeting will last;
   g. state your understanding of the initial purpose of the meeting;
   h. identify some of things you will do;
   i. identify what you expect your client to do;
   j. if appropriate, discuss agency policies and ethical and/or legal guidelines that will govern your behavior; and
   k. ask if your client has any questions.

3. Pretend this is a first appointment. Review the behaviors you will use to communicate involvement and what you need to observe in the client. As the practitioner, make your beginning statement to the client.

4. During the interview, the peer supervisor will watch the practitioner's use of behaviors that communicate involvement, observe the client, and check each item completed on the beginning process evaluation list.

The following activities will be completed after the interview:

5.   The client will share how he/she experienced the practitioner.

6.   The practitioner will evaluate her/his use of a beginning statement.

7.   As before, the peer supervisor will ask the practitioner to describe what he/she observed and will complete the evaluation form.

8.   The peer supervisor will complete the evaluation scale related to the beginning process skills.

Beginning Process Evaluation Scale

Level 1:   The practitioner begins without foundation for the meeting, covering none of the necessary elements.

Level 2:   The practitioner begins with minimal foundation for the meeting, covering two or three of the necessary elements.

Level 3:   The practitioner begins with a moderate foundation for the meeting, covering four or five of the necessary elements.

Level 4:   The practitioner covers all the necessary elements of the foundation for the meeting but appears rote.

Level 5:   The practitioner provides a foundation built on a clear understanding of such things as purpose, roles, and expectations for the meeting and appears focused on the client.

Using the scale, the peer supervisor will evaluate how well the practitioner creates a solid foundation by establishing a clear understanding of the purpose, roles, and expectations for the meeting.

9.   Continue until each person has been in each role.

An Example of a Possible Beginning Statement

Hello, my name is Valerie Chang. I am a social worker here at the ABC agency. I understand your name is Mrs. Smith. Did I pronounce your name correctly? Would you prefer using first or last names? Since you prefer first names, please call me Valerie.

Today, we will be meeting here in my office for ten minutes to discuss the challenges you are facing. I will be listening to you and asking you some questions in order to understand your situation. I will summarize what I am hearing to be sure that I have understood you accurately. Even though you just met me, I hope that you will decide to be

open and honest as you tell me about the challenges you are facing. How does that sound to you? If you have any questions either now or at any time, I hope you will bring them up.

I want you to know that everything you say to me will remain confidential within the agency unless you give me written permission to share information with someone else. The only exceptions to the confidentiality rule is if you tell me something that represents danger to yourself or another person. Such information will not be kept confidential. Would you like to talk more about the issue of confidentiality?

Beginning Process Evaluation Form

Name of Practitioner_____

Name of Peer Supervisor_____

<u>Directions</u>: Under each category (in italics) is a list of behaviors or skills. Give one point for each specific behavior or skill exhibited by the practitioner. On the scales, circle the number that best represents your evaluation of the appropriateness, effectiveness, or completeness of the practitioner's overall use of the skills or behaviors in the category.

<u>Basic Interpersonal Skills</u>
Communicating Involvement: Give one point for each behavior used by the practitioner. Using the scale, circle the number that represents your evaluation of the effectiveness of the practitioner's overall use of behaviors that communicate involvement.

1.	Open and accessible body posture	_____
2.	Congruent facial expression	_____
3.	Slightly inclined toward the client	_____
4.	Directly face the client	_____
4.	Regular eye contact unless inappropriate	_____
5.	No distracting behavior	_____
6.	Minimal encouragement	_____

1   2   3   4   5
Ineffective   Highly Effective

Observing: The practitioner will describe the client. Give one point for each item described accurately. Using the scale, circle the number that best represents your evaluation of the overall completeness of the practitioner's descriptions.

1.	Facial expression	_____
2.	Eye movement and contact	_____
3.	Body position and movement	_____
4.	Breathing patterns	_____
5.	Muscle tone	_____
6.	Gestures	_____
7.	Skin tone changes	_____

1   2   3   4   5
Incomplete   Complete

Beginning Process Skills: Give one point for each topic covered by the practitioner. Using the scale, circle the number that best represents your evaluation of the appropriateness and effectiveness of the practitioner's use of beginning skills.

1. Introduce yourself and your role _____
2. Seek introductions _____
3. Identify where meeting will be held _____
4. Identify how long meeting will last _____
5. Describe the initial purpose of the meeting _____
6. Explain some of the things you will do _____
7. Outline the client's role _____
8. Discuss ethical and agency policies _____
9. Seek feedback from the client _____

<u>Beginning Process Evaluation Scale</u>

Level 1: The practitioner begins without foundation for the meeting, covering none of the necessary elements.

Level 2: The practitioner begins with minimal foundation for the meeting, covering two or three of the necessary elements.

Level 3: The practitioner begins with a moderate foundation for the meeting, covering four or five of the necessary elements.

Level 4: The practitioner covers all the necessary elements of the foundation for the meeting but appears rote.

Level 5: The practitioner provides a foundation built on a clear understanding of such things as purpose, roles, and expectations for the meeting and appears focused on the client.

1	2	3	4	5
Ineffective &/or Inappropriate				Highly Effective or Appropriate

Total Score: Add each point and each circled number to get the total score for the interview.

_____
Score

III

EXPLORING PROCESS

In order to fully understand the problems or challenges, the person, and the situation, the practitioner will use many skills. Expressing empathic understanding is a critical skill in any effective interviewing process. Empathy involves understanding another person's experience, behavior, and feelings and communicating that understanding to the other person.

Unfortunately, we rarely really listen to each other and even more rarely express our understanding, so this interviewing skill is new for most people. Students often express feeling awkward and uncomfortable expressing their understanding. Sometimes, students assume that their clients know that they are listening and understand. Remember, your clients have no way of knowing you are listening unless you express your understanding of what you have heard. Often, you will find that your understanding is not exactly what your client meant. Only by your expressing your understanding do you give your client an opportunity to further elaborate, explain, or correct your restatement.

The meaning of an event or situation or problem may not be obvious in the content. "It is always implicit but not always explicit" (Carkhuff & Anthony, 1979, p. 72). To understand meanings, you need to observe of the behavior and tone that accompanies the content. For example, if your client says, "I've never talked this much with a white woman, but I guess it will be okay." While saying this, you notice that your client looks concerned or scared and is ringing her hands. Your observations would probably lead you to say, "I can understand that it might be hard to talk with someone who seems so different from yourself. Let's begin by talking about what it is like for you to be talking to me."

When working with clients that come from a different background, culture, ethnicity, or experience from yours, it is particularly important to continually express your understandings by giving your clients a chance to further explain what they have expressed. You will want to explore what these differences might mean to your client and how they might affect your relationship.

Consciously dealing with diversity variables when developing relationships can make your job easier, not more difficult. Research suggests that having a similar world view is more important to many clients than such differences as age, ethnicity, race, gender, sexual orientation, and physical differences. However, for some clients the more obvious differences between you may be a barrier to your developing an empathic relationship. Also, you may or may not be speaking in their native language. This will obviously influence the nature of your communication and perhaps your ability to understand each other either literally or in terms of the way words are used. Sensitivity to these issues and the meaning that the client gives to them will provide a framework for the other types of exploring you will do together.

In this section you will focus on the following skills: Reflecting Feelings, Reflecting Content, Reflecting Feeling and Content, Using Questions, Seeking Clarification, and Advanced Reflecting. Expressing your understanding of what the client has communicated has been called reflecting, responding, restating, and summarizing. Using these skills you will be reaching to understand your client's feelings, thoughts, opinions, points of view, values and expectations, world view, situation, and challenges. When your clients feel understood, they are likely to be willing to continue telling you about their situation and further explore their challenges. In this unit, you will practice using reflecting skills to invite your clients to explore further and to express your understanding of your client. You will also learn to use questions to invite your clients to focus on particular areas, to seek clarification on specific areas, or to fill out any of their descriptions.

Along with your increasing ability to use basic practice skills, you will begin to focus on the core interpersonal qualities of warmth, respect, empathy, and genuineness. Rogers (1957; 1961) proposed that these basic qualities or attitudes are essential for the development of good working relationships between clients and practitioners. Generally, as you become more comfortable using the skills, you will be able to relax and communicate warmth, respect, empathy, and genuineness more easily.

Written Exercise A: Identifying Feeling and Content Statements

Objective of Exercise: To learn to differentiate expressions of thoughts from expressions of feelings. In order to express your empathic understanding of your client, it is important for you to be a good communicator. In our society, people often avoid expressing how they feel and confuse expressions of thoughts with expressions of feelings. For example, if I say, "I feel like you don't like me." I am expressing a thought. I could change that to a feeling and thought statement by saying, "I feel sad because I think you don't like me."

Directions: Listed below are five pairs of statements. One statement in each pair contains the person's feeling and reason for that feeling, while the other expresses the person's thoughts or opinions. Check the feeling statements. This homework should be completed before doing the practice exercise on reflecting skills.

1. _____ I feel that my husband ought to help with the kids.
   __✔__ I feel annoyed because it seems to me that my husband should help with the kids and he doesn't.

2. _____ I feel like my mother-in-law comes around too much.
   __✔__ I get unhappy because I think my mother-in-law comes around too much.

3. __✔__ When my boss gives me more work than the others, I get resentful.
   _____ I feel my boss is unfair because he gives me more work than the others.

4. _____ I feel that the students in this class are working hard.
   __✔__ I feel pleased that the students in this class are doing well.

5. __✔__ I feel worried that several nurses on this unity aren't keeping up with the new technology.
   _____ I feel that nurses should be motivated to learn new things.

Written Exercise B: Writing Feeling and Content Statements

Objective of Exercise: To learn to move from thought statements to statements that reflect the possible feelings related to the thoughts. As a practitioner, it will be important for you to understand what your client thinks and how she/he feels. With clients who express their thoughts and not their feelings, you will need to express your empathic understanding of their thoughts and feelings.

Directions: Listed below are thought statements. Rewrite the statement so that it includes both a feeling and related thought. Use the format "You seem to be feeling _____ because _____." For example, if your client said, "You aren't listening to me." You might say, "You seem to be feeling mad because you believe that I am not listening to you." In this exercise, you do not have any observational clues to help you guess what the client might be feeling so put yourself in the client's position and express how you might be feeling in that situation. This homework should be completed before doing the practice exercise on reflecting skills.

1. My son is totally insensitive to my feelings.

you seem to be feeling frustrated that your son does not seem to care about your feelings

2. This school demands too much of the students.

You seem to be feeling overwhelmed because you believe this school demands too much of the student

3. The doctor I am seeing has no bedside manner. He is always in a hurry.

you seem to be feeling angry with your doctor for not taking enough time with you

4. My teachers expect too much from me.

You seem to be feeling overwhelmed that your teachers expect you to do more than you can get done

5. My mother treats me like a child.

You seem to be feeling unhappy that your mother does not appear to treat you as an adult

6. The other nurses on this ward don't seem to care about the patients.

You seem to be feeling resentful that the other nurses are caring enough about the patients

28

7. My co-workers aren't doing their share.

You seem to be feeling resentful that it seems like your co-workers aren't doing as much as you

8. My best friend is always late.

You seem to be feeling angry with your best friend for being late

9. Last weekend my teenage son was two hours late. He told me later that he decided to go out for pizza after the movie. I thought he had been in an accident. Kids are so inconsiderate.

You seem to be feeling irritated with your son when he does not let you know where he is.

10. My wife spends money without thinking. We got a notice in the mail yesterday that the check to Sears bounced. She is always doing that.

You seem to be feeling angry for writing checks that bounce

11. My son acts so silly when my friends come over.

You seem to be feeling irritated with your son for being silly when your friends come over

12. My secretary never gets reports in on time.

You seem to be feeling frustrated with your secretary for not getting reports in on time

13. One of the people in my group just isn't doing his share of the work.

You seem to be feeling resentful that one of the people in your group is doing less work than the others

14. My wife just doesn't listen to me.

You seem to be feeling unhappy with your wife since she doesn't listen to you

15. The people in my church seem to want me to take responsibility for everything.

You seem to be feeling frustrated that people in your church so often look to you to take responsibility for things.

16. I wish my friend had invited me to the party.

You seem to be feeling left out since your friend did not invite you to the party

29

Inappropriate Responses

Although a goal of always being effective is not achievable, you can set a goal of not being inappropriate. You have probably used inappropriate responses before taking this class. Most of us use some destructive responses in our attempt to be helpful or out of our frustration and need to change a situation or a person.

The following responses are inappropriate:

- *Moralizing, sermonizing, lecturing, instructing, persuading, arguing, intellectualizing, threatening, or warning, and using words like "should," and "ought."* Unless your role is parent, teacher, or something similar and the person is asking for direction or instruction, this type of communication tends to invite the other person to feel one-down or rebellious. They will probably either want to argue or withdraw from you.

- *Advising prematurely.* Asking leading questions, such as "have you considered asking your professor about that?" is the same as advising. Your client will probably understand your question as telling him/her to talk to the professor. Remember the last time you were troubled and wanted to tell someone about your situation. I bet that what you wanted was for the other person to listen to you. If instead, they told you what to do how would you feel? If you had wanted suggestions about what to do, I am sure that you would have asked for suggestions. The same is true of your clients. If they want advice, they will ask. Remember that you learn a great deal from figuring something out on your own. The only way to gain a sense of empowerment or personal capacity is by doing it yourself. Of course, you have lots of great ideas about how to solve someone else's problem, but before you start offering your ideas be sure that you know exactly what the other person's goal is and that you at least ask them if they want your suggestions. Even then, remember that by offering your ideas you are the one that gets to feel smart and capable not your client. Do not act like a surrogate frontal lobe for your clients (Meichenbaum & Turk, 1987), instead be selective in the information or advice given.

- *Judging, hostilely criticizing, or blaming.* Do you find it helpful for someone to judge, criticize, or blame you? This type of communication invites the other person to feel less important than you. Frequently, they respond with anger, defensiveness, or sadness.

- *Analyzing, diagnosing, making glib interpretations, or labeling behavior.* These types of communication are sophisticated ways of judging, criticizing, or blaming.

- *Reassuring, sympathizing, consoling, excusing.* It is essential that you be empathic, but not sympathetic. Sympathy comes from a one-up position. Think about times when someone has been sympathetic with you. Did you feel like under what they were saying was an implied, "You poor darling?" How did you feel about the sympathy that was offered to you? Reassuring is another type of communication that sounds nice, but is not helpful. Unless you are sure that you can predict the future and know that "it will all be okay," it is not beneficial to be reassuring. Saying things that sound consoling or advise giving but are impossible to do is not constructive. For example, think of all the times someone has told you, "Don't worry about it." Good idea, but if you knew how to stop worrying I am sure you would have stopped.

- *Gallows laughter.* Unfortunately, in our society gallows laughter, or laughing about things that are not funny, is very common. Think about times when you have heard people laugh about getting drunk, being hurt, making mistakes, or being embarrassed. If as a practitioner you laugh, you are supporting the hurtful or painful behavior.

- *Shifting the focus to yourself.* Although there are time when you will use self disclosure, that will only be done to share your response to a here and now situation or to briefly express understanding based on personal experience. With few exceptions, the focus should be on your client.

- *Habitual poor communication patterns.* Using phrases repetitively without thinking, for example, "okay" or "you know" can led to misunderstanding. These are communication habits that invite misunderstanding. When you unconsciously say "okay," it is in fact permission giving. The problem is that you probably did not consciously mean to be giving permission. "You know" actually indicates that you believe the other person understands or has information about the subject. If that is not the situation, your unconscious use of "you know" can invite misunderstanding. As practitioners, it is important that you be very clear communicators particularly in today's world in which you will be working with people from many different backgrounds and cultures. Using the phrase "I feel" when you are going to discuss your thoughts, opinions, beliefs, values, and/or judgements is very common in our society, but it invites misunderstanding. If I say, "I feel that you are doing fine work in this class." I am telling you about what I think not what I feel.

Skill-Building 5: Reflecting

Objective of Exercise: To practice expressing your understanding of what your client is communicating by responding to client statements by reflecting feeling and content and to practice expressing warmth and concern in appropriate and effective ways.

Directions for Exercise:

1.   Form groups of three people. You will each play the roles of the practitioner, client, and peer supervisor.

2.   Each practitioner/client session will be ten minutes long.

3.   The client will discuss a problem. These exercises will be much more authentic if you talk from your own experience. Consider discussing a problem that happened to you in the past and may be resolved. Remember, the goal is for the practitioner to practice her/his skills. It is helpful if as client you pause after every few sentences to allow the practitioner a chance to respond.

4.   The practitioner will communicate involvement, observe, start with a beginning statement, and listen carefully.

5.   The practitioner will also make statements that reflect feeling, content, and/or feeling and content or meaning.

6.   During the interview, the peer supervisor will watch the practitioner's use of behaviors that communicate involvement, observe the client, listen to the client, give one point for each item completed on the beginning process list, and keep track of time. In order to evaluate the practitioner's statements, the peer supervisor will write down each of the practitioner's statements after the beginning statement. Writing out each practitioner statement is very difficult but critical in order to effectively evaluate the practitioner's work. In all future interviews, the peer supervisor will be asked to write out each statement made by the practitioner. You may have to abbreviate, use your own form of shorthand, or just write the first group of words in the statement; but do the best you can to get the essence of what the practitioner says. Without a written record there is no way for you to accurately identify statements and give solid feedback.

The following activities will be completed after the interview:

7. The client will share how he/she experienced the practitioner.

8. The practitioner will evaluate her/his use of reflecting skills.

9. The peer supervisor will ask the practitioner to describe what he/she observed and heard from the client and to summarize what the client said. The peer supervisor will evaluate the practitioner's use of activities that communicate involvement, the practitioner's ability to accurately observe, and the practitioner's use of active listening skills and beginning process skills. All the evaluation scales are in Appendix A at the end of the book.

10. The peer supervisor will go over each response and give one point for each type of reflective response used by the practitioner.

11. The peer supervisor will evaluate how well the practitioner used reflecting skills using the reflecting skill evaluation scale.

Reflecting Skills Evaluation Scale

Level 1: The practitioner makes very little attempt to verbalize understanding of content, feelings, and meanings.

Level 2: The practitioner minimally verbalizes understanding of feelings, content, and/or meanings.

Level 3: The practitioner moderately verbalizes understanding of feelings, content, and/or meanings..

Level 4: The practitioner generally verbalizes understanding of feelings, content, and/or meanings.

Level 5: The practitioner consistently verbalizes understanding of feelings, content, and/or meanings.

Using the scale, the peer supervisor will evaluate how consistently the practitioner verbalizes understanding of content, feelings, and/or meanings.

12. The peer supervisor will evaluate how well the practitioner expressed the core interpersonal competency of warmth.

Warmth Evaluation Scale

Level 1: The practitioner is cold, detached, and/or mechanical displaying no concern for the client.

Level 2: The practitioner is generally detached or mechanical displaying only minimal concern and compassion for the client.

Level 3: The practitioner shows some concern and compassion for the client.

Level 4:   The practitioner generally shows concern and compassion for the client.
Level 5:   The practitioner communicates verbal and nonverbal expressions of concern and compassion that are appropriately suited to the unique needs of the client.

Using the scale, the peer supervisor will evaluate how effectively the practitioner is able to communicate warmth to the client.

13.   Starting with this interview, the peer supervisor will identify any inappropriate responses and give the practitioner minus one point for each inappropriate response.

14.   Continue until each person has been in each role.

Reflecting Evaluation Form

Name of Practitioner_____

Name of Peer Supervisor_____

Directions: Under each category (in italics) is a list of behaviors or skills. Give one point for each specific behavior or skill exhibited by the practitioner. On the scales, circle the number that best represents your evaluation of the appropriateness, effectiveness, or completeness of the practitioner's overall use of the skills or behaviors in the category.

Basic Interpersonal Skills

Communicating Involvement: Give one point for each behavior used by the practitioner. Using the scale, circle the number that represents your evaluation of the effectiveness of the practitioner's overall use of behaviors that communicate involvement.

1.   Open and accessible body posture   _____
2.   Congruent facial expression   _____
3.   Slightly inclined toward the client   _____
4.   Directly face the client   _____
4.   Regular eye contact unless inappropriate _____
5.   No distracting behavior   _____
6.   Minimal encouragement   _____

1	2	3	4	5
Ineffective				Highly Effective

Observing: The practitioner will describe the client. Give one point for each item described accurately. Using the scale, circle the number that best represents your evaluation of the overall completeness of the practitioner's descriptions.

1.   Facial expression   _____
2.   Eye movement and contact   _____
3.   Body position and movement   _____
4.   Breathing patterns   _____
5.   Muscle tone   _____
6.   Gestures   _____
7.   Skin tone changes   _____

1	2	3	4	5
Incomplete				Complete

35

Active Listening Skills—Content and Process: Using the scale, circle the number that best represents your evaluation of the accuracy and completeness of the practitioner's summary of what the client said and description of the client's way of speaking including speaking style, vocal tone and volume, and speed of delivery.

1	2	3	4	5
Incomplete				Complete

Beginning Process Skills: Give one point for each topic covered by the practitioner. Using the scale, circle the number that best represents your evaluation of the appropriateness and effectiveness of the practitioner's use of beginning skills.

1. Introduce yourself and your role   _____
2. Seek introductions   _____
3. Identify where meeting will be held   _____
4. Identify how long meeting will last   _____
5. Describe the initial purpose of the meeting   _____
6. Explain some of the things you will do   _____
7. Outline the client's role   _____
8. Discuss ethical and agency policies   _____
9. Seek feedback from the client   _____

1	2	3	4	5
Ineffective &/or Inappropriate				Highly Effective & Appropriate

Exploring Process

Advanced Reflecting Skills: Give one point for each skill used by the practitioner. Using the scale, circle the number that best represents your evaluation of the appropriateness and effectiveness of the practitioner's use of reflecting skills.

1. Reflecting content   _____
2. Reflecting feelings   _____
3. Reflecting feeling, content, and/or meaning   _____

Reflecting Skills Evaluation Scale

Level 1:   The practitioner makes very little attempt to verbalize understanding of content, feelings, and meanoings.

Level 2:   The practitioner minimally verbalizes understanding of content, feelings, and/or meanings.

Level 3:   The practitioner verbalizes some understanding of content, feelings, and/or meanings.

Level 4:   The practitioner generally verbalizes understanding of content, feelings, and meanings.

Level 5:   The practitioner consistently verbalizes understanding of content, feelings, and meanings.

1	2	3	4	5
Ineffective &/or Inappropriate				Highly Effective & Appropriate

Core Interpersonal Quality

Using the scale, evaluate the appropriateness and effectiveness of the practitioner's use of warmth.   Circle the number that best represents your evaluation of the practitioner's expression of warmth.

Warmth Evaluation Scale

Level 1:   The practitioner is cold, detached, and/or mechanical displaying no concern for the client.

Level 2:   The practitioner is generally detached or mechanical displaying only minimal concern and compassion for the client.

Level 3:   The practitioner shows some concern and compassion for the client.

Level 4:   The practitioner generally shows concern and compassion for the client.

Level 5:   The practitioner communicates verbal and nonverbal expressions of concern and compassion that are appropriately suited to the unique needs of the client.

1	2	3	4	5
Ineffective &/or Inappropriate				Highly Effective & Appropriate

Overall Effectiveness of Practitioner Communication

Inappropriate Statements: Minus one point for each statement.   _____

Total Score: Add each point and each circled number to get the total score for the interview.

_____
Score

Skill-Building 6: Questioning

Objective of Exercise: To practice using questions to gain further information. After expressing your empathic understanding of your client, you may decide to ask a question to direct the client to focus on a particular area or to expand or to clarify something. Areas of possible exploration include: what are the clients strengths, how do they see their problems, why are they are seeking help now, and what type of help do they want. Open-ended questions invite your client to broadly explore a particular topic. Close-ended questions invite your client to give you a specific piece of information. You should chose the type of question to use based on your goal at the time.

Whatever type of question you use, be sure to use no more than one question at a time. As you know from your own experience, multiple questions are confusing. Use of multiple questions also can lead to you losing control of the direction of the interview.

Directions for Exercise:

1. Form groups of three people. You will each play the roles of the practitioner, client, and peer supervisor.

2. Each practitioner/client session will be ten minutes long.

3. The client will identify and discuss a problem. Even though you may be a very verbal person, allow openings or stop talking to give the practitioner a chance to practice using reflecting skills and asking questions.

4. The practitioner will communicate involvement, observe, start with a beginning statement, listen carefully, and reflect feelings, content, and/ or meanings.

5. The practitioner will ask questions to more clearly define and understand the problems or challenges, the person, and the situation. The following questions are examples of ones you might chose to us:
   a. When did the problem begin?
   b. What have you already done to try to solve the problem?
   c. How often does the problem occur?
   d. How has the problem affected your general functioning?
   e. How do you feel about having this problem?
   f. What other people are affected by your problem?
   g. What led you to come discuss this problem with me now?

6. During the interview, the peer supervisor will watch the practitioner's use of behaviors that communicate involvement, observe the client, listen to the client, check each item completed on the beginning process list, and keep track of time. In order to evaluate each of the practitioner's responses, the peer supervisor will write down each response after the beginning statement.

The following activities will be completed after the interview:

7. The client will share how he/she experienced the practitioner.

8. The practitioner will evaluate her/his use of questioning skills.

9. The peer supervisor will ask the practitioner to describe what he/she observed and heard from the client and ask the practitioner to summarize what the client said. The peer supervisor will evaluate the practitioner's use of activities that communicate involvement, the practitioner's ability to accurately observe, the practitioner's active listening skills, beginning process skills, and reflecting skills and check for any use of inappropriate responses. The peer supervisor will also evaluate the practitioner's use of the core interpersonal quality of warmth.

10. The peer supervisor will evaluate the practitioner's use of questions. Give one point for each questioning skill used by the practitioner.

11. The peer supervisor will evaluate the appropriateness of the practitioner's use of questions.

Questioning Evaluation Scale

Level 1:   The practitioner uses questions ineffectively and/or inappropriately, uses multiple questions, or overuses questions.
Level 2:   The practitioner's appropriate use of questions is minimal, sometimes uses multiple questions, and/or occasionally overuses questions.
Level 3:   The practitioner usually uses questions appropriately, does not ask multiple questions, and usually does not overuse questions.
Level 4:   The practitioner's use of questions is mostly effective and appropriate, with no multiple questions, and only occasional overuses questions.
Level 5:   The practitioner consistently uses questions effectively and appropriately.

Use the scale to evaluate how effectively the practitioner used questions.

12. The peer supervisor will evaluate the level of clarity or specificity of

information about the problem(s) or challenge(s), the person, and the situation that was included in the session. This information may be shared by the client or the practitioner may have to ask about a particular area. Use the evaluation scales on the person, the problem(s) and the situation to complete this part of the evaluation.

Problems or Challenges Evaluation Scale
Level 1:   Little or no information is discussed about the problem(s).
Level 2:   Minimal information is discussed about one or two aspects of the problem(s).
Level 3:   Three aspects of the problem(s) are discussed adequately but not fully.
Level 4:   All four aspects of the problem(s) are discussed adequately but not fully.
Level 5:   Full and complete information about all four aspects of the problem(s) are discussed.

Person Evaluation Scale
Level 1:   Little or no information is discussed about the person(s).
Level 2:   Minimal information is discussed about one aspects of the person(s).
Level 3:   Two aspects of the person(s) are discussed adequately but not fully.
Level 4:   All three aspects of the person(s) are discussed adequately but not fully.
Level 5:   Full and complete information about three aspects of the person(s) are discussed.

Situation Evaluation Scale
Level 1:   Little or no information is discussed about the situation.
Level 2:   Minimal information is discussed about the situation.
Level 3:   Moderate information is discussed about the situation.
Level 4:   Most aspects of information about the situation are discussed.
Level 5:   Full and complete information about the four aspects of the situation are discussed.

13.   Continue until each person has been in each role.

Questioning Evaluation Form

Name of Practitioner_____

Name of Peer Supervisor_____

Directions: Under each category (in italics) is a list of behaviors or skills. Give one point for each specific behavior or skill exhibited by the practitioner. On the scales, circle the number that best represents your evaluation of the appropriateness, effectiveness, or completeness of the practitioner's overall use of the skills or behaviors in the category.

Basic Interpersonal Skills

Communicating Involvement: Give one point for each behavior used by the practitioner. Using the scale, circle the number that represents your evaluation of the effectiveness of the practitioner's overall use of behaviors that communicate involvement.

1.	Open and accessible body posture	_____
2.	Congruent facial expression	_____
3.	Slightly inclined toward the client	_____
4.	Directly face the client	_____
4.	Regular eye contact unless inappropriate	_____
5.	No distracting behavior	_____
6.	Minimal encouragement	_____

1   2   3   4   5

Ineffective   Highly Effective

Observing: The practitioner will describe the client. Give one point for each item described accurately. Using the scale, circle the number that best represents your evaluation of the overall completeness of the practitioner's descriptions.

1.	Facial expression	_____
2.	Eye movement and contact	_____
3.	Body position and movement	_____
4.	Breathing patterns	_____
5.	Muscle tone	_____
6.	Gestures	_____
7.	Skin tone changes	_____

1   2   3   4   5

Incomplete   Complete

Active Listening Skills, Content and Process: Using the scale, circle the number that best represents your evaluation of the accuracy and completeness of the practitioner's summary of what the client said and description of the client's way of speaking including speaking style, vocal tone and volume, and speed of delivery.

1	2	3	4	5
Incomplete				Complete

Beginning Process Skills: Give one point for each topic covered by the practitioner. Using the scale, circle the number that best represents your evaluation of the appropriateness and effectiveness of the practitioner's use of beginning skills.

1. Introduce yourself and your role   _____
2. Seek introductions   _____
3. Identify where meeting will be held   _____
4. Identify how long meeting will last   _____
5. Describe the initial purpose of the meeting _____
6. Explain some of the things you will do   _____
7. Outline the client's role   _____
8. Discuss ethical and agency policies   _____
9. Seek feedback from the client   _____

1	2	3	4	5
Ineffective &/or Inappropriate				Highly Effective & Appropriate

<u>Exploring Process</u>

Reflecting Skills: Give one point for each skill used by the practitioner. Using the scale, circle the number that best represents your evaluation of the appropriateness and effectiveness of the practitioner's use of reflecting skills.

1. Reflecting content   _____
2. Reflecting feelings   _____
3. Reflecting feeling, content, and/or meaning _____

1	2	3	4	5
Ineffective &/or Inappropriate				Highly Effective & Appropriate

Questioning Skills: Give one point for each skill used by the practitioner. Using the scale, circle the number that best represents your evaluation of the appropriateness and effectiveness of the practitioner's use of questioning skills.

1. Use of open-ended questions   _____
2. Use of one question at a time   _____
3. Correct use of closed-ended questions   _____

Questioning Evaluation Scale

Level 1: The practitioner uses questions ineffectively and/or inappropriately, uses multiple questions, or overuses questions.

Level 2: The practitioner's appropriate use of questions is minimal, sometimes uses multiple questions, and/or occasionally overuses questions.

Level 3: The practitioner usually uses questions appropriately, does not ask multiple questions, and usually does not overuse questions.

Level 4: The practitioner's use of questions is mostly effective and appropriate, with no multiple questions and only occasional overuses questions.

Level 5: The practitioner consistently uses questions effectively and appropriately.

1	2	• 3	4	5

Ineffective &/or
Inappropriate

Highly Effective &
Appropriate

1. **Problems or Challenges**

   Previous attempts to solve problem(s) _____

   History of the problem(s) _____

   Precipitating factors _____

   Severity or intensity of the problem _____

Problem(s) or Challenges Evaluation Scale

Level 1: Little or no information is discussed about the problem(s).

Level 2: Minimal information is discussed about one or two aspects of the problem(s).

Level 3: Three aspects of the problem(s) are discussed adequately but not fully.

Level 4: All four aspects of the problem(s) are discussed adequately but not fully.

Level 5: Full and complete information about all four aspects of the problem(s) are discussed.

1	2	3	4	5

No Information

Complete Information

2. **Person**

   Feelings about having the problem(s) _____

   Effect of the problem(s) on functioning _____

   Personal strengths _____

Person Evaluation Scale

Level 1: Little or no information is discussed about the person(s).

Level 2: Minimal information is discussed about one aspects of the person(s).

Level 3: Two aspects of the person(s) are discussed adequately but not fully.

Level 4: All three aspects of the person(s) are discussed adequately but not fully.

Level 5: Full and complete information about three aspects of the person(s) is discussed.

1	2	3	4	5
No Information				Complete Information

3. **Situation**
   Effect of the problem(s) on others   _____
   Available social support   _____
   Demands and stresses in the situation/environment   _____
   Strengths in the situation/environment   _____

Situation Evaluation Scale

Level 1: Little or no information is discussed about the situation.
Level 2: Minimal information is discussed about one or two aspects of the situation.
Level 3: Three aspects of the situation are discussed adequately but not fully.
Level 4: All four aspects of the problem are discussed adequately but not fully.
Level 5: Full and complete information about all four aspects of the situation is discussed.

1	2	3	4	5
No Information				Complete Information

Core Interpersonal Quality

Using the scale, evaluate the appropriateness and effectiveness of the practitioner's use of warmth. Circle the number that best represents your evaluation of the practitioner's expression of warmth.

Warmth

1	2	3	4	5
Ineffective &/or Inappropriate				Highly Effective & Appropriate

Overall Effectiveness of Practitioner Communication

Inappropriate Statements: Minus one point for each statement.   _____

Total Score Add each point and each circled number to get the total score for the interview.

                                _____
                                Score

Skill-Building 7: Seeking Clarification

Objective of Exercise: To practice using statements and asking questions to seek clarification and to gain specific information and to practice showing respect for your client. We often communicate with each other in a shorthand way. We assume that the other person uses words in the same way we do, that the other can somehow fill in the information we leave out, that the other person understands how we have come to conclusions, and that the other person understands our interaction with other people. This type of communication leads to misunderstanding. As a practitioner, it is important that you listen for the gaps in information and notice the points of lack of clarity. In your attempt to fully understand your client, you may chose to ask your client to elaborate or be more specific. Remember to allow time for your client to explain before jumping in with a question.

Directions for Exercise:

1. Form groups of three people. You will each play the roles of the practitioner, client, and peer supervisor.

2. Each practitioner/client session will be ten minutes long.

3. The client will discuss a problem.

4. The practitioner will communicate involvement, observe, start with a beginning statement, listen carefully, reflect feelings, content, and/or meanings, and use questions to gain an understanding of the problem(s) or challenge(s), person, and situation.

5. The practitioner will also use questions to seek clarification
    a. Clarifying the meaning of words and phrases (e.g., "In what way is he mean to you?").
    b. Exploring the basis of conclusions drawn by the client (e.g., "What leads you to think that he is planning to leave you?")
    c. Eliciting further clarifying information (e.g., "Do you mean . . .?" or "Are you saying . . .?").
    d. Eliciting details regarding interaction (e.g., "Then what happened?" or "What did you say before that?").

6. During the interview, the peer supervisor will watch the practitioner's use of behaviors that communicate involvement, observe the client, listen to the client, check each item completed on the beginning process list, and keep track of time. In order to evaluate the practitioner's responses, the peer supervisor will write down each practitioner response after the beginning statement.

The following activities will be completed after the interview:

7. The client will share how he/she experienced the practitioner.

8. The practitioner will evaluate her/his use of responses that seek clarification.

9. The peer supervisor will go over each response and give one point for each type of skill used by the practitioner.

10. The peer supervisor will ask the practitioner to describe what he/she observed and heard from the client and will ask the practitioner to summarize what the client said. The peer supervisor will evaluate the practitioner's use of activities that communicate involvement, the practitioner's ability to accurately observe, the practitioner's active listening skills, beginning process skills, reflecting skills, and questioning skills and check for any use of inappropriate responses. He/she will evaluate how well information about the problem(s) or challenge(s), the person, and the situation was covered.

11. The peer supervisor will evaluate seeking clarification skills.

Seeking Clarification Evaluation Scale
Level 1:   The practitioner does very little to invite understanding of the client's reality.
Level 2:   The practitioner is sometimes able to use questions to invite some understanding of the client's reality.
Level 3:   The practitioner is generally able to use questions to invite some understanding of the client's reality.
Level 4:   The practitioner mostly is able to use questions to invite full understanding of the client's reality, including such things as exploring the meaning of words or gestures, the basis of conclusions, and the process of interactions and apparent contradictions.
Level 5:   The practitioner uses questions to invite full understanding of the client's reality, including such things as exploring the meaning of words or gestures, the basis of conclusions, and the process of interactions and apparent contradictions.

Using this scale, the peer supervisor will evaluate how well the practitioner uses questions to invite full understanding of the client's reality.

12. The peer supervisor will evaluate the practitioner's use of the core interpersonal qualities of warmth and respect.

<u>Respect Evaluation Scale</u>

Level 1:   The practitioner communicates that the client's feelings and thoughts are not valid or important and/or communicates a belief that the client is not capable.

Level 2:   The practitioner communicates that the client's feelings, thoughts, potential, and ability to solve problems are not valid or limited.

Level 3:   The practitioner communicates regard for the client's feelings, thoughts and potential.

Level 4:   The practitioner communicates regard for the client's feelings, thoughts, and potential and sometimes invites the client to identify strengths, resources, and capacities that can be used to achieve goals.

Level 5:   The practitioner communicates regard for the client's feelings, thoughts, potential, and worth as a person and invites the client to identify strengths, resources, and capacities that can be used to achieve goals.

Using this scale, the peer supervisor will evaluate how well the practitioner communicates regard for the client's feelings, thoughts, potential, and worth as well as how well the practitioner invites the client to identify strengths, resources, and capacities.

13.   Continue until each person has been in each role.

Seeking Clarification Evaluation Form

Name of Practitioner_____

Name of Peer Supervisor_____

<u>Directions</u>: Under each category (in italics) is a list of behaviors or skills. Give one point for each specific behavior or skill exhibited by the practitioner. On the scales, circle the number that best represents your evaluation of the appropriateness, effectiveness, or completeness of the practitioner's overall use of the skills or behaviors in the category.

<u>Basic Interpersonal Skills</u>
Communicating Involvement: Give one point for each behavior used by the practitioner. Using the scale, circle the number that represents your evaluation of the effectiveness of the practitioner's overall use of behaviors that communicate involvement.

1.	Open and accessible body posture	_____
2.	Congruent facial expression	_____
3.	Slightly inclined toward the client	_____
4.	Directly face the client	_____
4.	Regular eye contact unless inappropriate	_____
5.	No distracting behavior	_____
6.	Minimal encouragement	_____

<u>1</u>   2   3   4   <u>5</u>
Ineffective   Highly Effective

Observing: The practitioner will describe the client. Give one point for each item described accurately. Using the scale, circle the number that best represents your evaluation of the overall completeness of the practitioner's descriptions.

1.	Facial expression	_____
2.	Eye movement and contact	_____
3.	Body position and movement	_____
4.	Breathing patterns	_____
5.	Muscle tone	_____
6.	Gestures	_____
7.	Skin tone changes	_____

<u>1</u>   2   3   4   <u>5</u>
Incomplete   Complete

Active Listening Skills—Content and Process: Using the scale, circle the number that best represents your evaluation of the accuracy and completeness of the practitioner's summary of what the client said and description of the client's way of speaking including speaking style, vocal tone and volume, and speed of delivery.

1	2	3	4	5
Incomplete				Complete

Beginning Process Skills: Give one point for each topic covered by the practitioner. Using the scale, circle the number that best represents your evaluation of the appropriateness and effectiveness of the practitioner's use of beginning skills.

1. Introduce yourself and your role   _____
2. Seek introductions   _____
3. Identify where meeting will be held   _____
4. Identify how long meeting will last   _____
5. Describe the initial purpose of the meeting   _____
6. Explain some of the things you will do   _____
7. Outline the client's role   _____
8. Discuss ethical and agency policies   _____
9. Seek feedback from the client   _____

1	2	3	4	5
Ineffective &/or Inappropriate				Highly Effective & Appropriate

Exploring Process

Reflecting Skills: Give one point for each skill used by the practitioner. Using the scale, circle the number that best represents your evaluation of the appropriateness and effectiveness of the practitioner's use of reflecting skills.

1. Reflecting content   _____
2. Reflecting feelings   _____
3. Reflecting feeling, content, and/or meaning   _____

1	2	3	4	5
Ineffective &/or Inappropriate				Highly Effective & Appropriate

Questioning Skills: Give one point for each skill used by the practitioner. Using the scale, circle the number that best represents your evaluation of the appropriateness and effectiveness of the practitioner's use of questioning skills.

1. Use of open-ended questions _____
2. Use of one question at a time _____
3. Correct use of closed-ended questions _____

1	2	3	4	5

Ineffective &/or   Highly Effective &
Inappropriate   Appropriate

Person, Problem/Challenge, and Situation Over Time Exploration: Give one point for each item covered. Using the scale, circle the number that best represents your evaluation of the level of clarity and completeness in each of the three areas.

1. <u>Problems or Challenges</u>
   Previous attempts to solve problem(s) _____
   History of the problem(s) _____
   Precipitating factors _____
   Severity or intensity of the problem(s) _____

1	2	3	4	5

No Information   Complete Information

2. <u>Person</u>
   Feelings about having the problem(s) _____
   Effect of the problem(s) on functioning _____
   Personal strengths _____

1	2	3	4	5

No Information   Complete Information

3. <u>Situation</u>
   Effect of the problem(s) on others _____
   Available social support _____
   Demands and stresses in the situation/environment _____
   Strengths in the situation/environment _____

1	2	3	4	5

No Information   Complete Information

Seeking Clarification: Give one point for each skill used by the practitioner. Using the scale, circle the number that best represents your evaluation of e the appropriateness and effectiveness of the practitioner's use of skills.

1. Exploring the meaning of words and body language _____
2. Exploring the basis of conclusions drawn by client _____
3. Exploring statements that appear contradictory _____
4. Exploring details regarding interaction _____

Seeking Clarification Evaluation Scale

Level 1: The practitioner does very little to invite understanding of the client's reality.

Level 2: The practitioner is sometimes able to use questions to invite some understanding of the client's reality.

Level 3: The practitioner is generally able to use questions to invite some understanding of the client's reality.

Level 4: The practitioner mostly is able to use questions to invite full understanding of the client's reality, including such things as exploring the meaning of words or gestures, the basis of conclusions, and the process of interactions and apparent contradictions.

Level 5: The practitioner uses questions to invite full understanding of the client's reality, including such things as exploring the meaning of words or gestures, the basis of conclusions, and the process of interactions and apparent contradictions.

```
1           2           3           4           5
```
Ineffective &/or   Highly Effective &
Inappropriate   Appropriate

Core Interpersonal Qualities

Using the scale, circle the number that best represents the practitioner's use of each quality.

Warmth
```
1           2           3           4           5
```
Ineffective &/or   Highly Effective &
Inappropriate   Appropriate

Respect Evaluation Scale

Level 1: The practitioner communicates that the client's feelings and thoughts are not valid or important and/or communicates a belief that the client is not capable.

Level 2: The practitioner communicates that the client's feelings, thoughts, potential, and ability to solve problems are not valid or limited.

Level 3: The practitioner communicates regard for the client's feelings, thoughts, and potential.

Level 4: The practitioner communicates regard for the client's feelings, thoughts, and potential and sometimes invites the client to identify strengths, resources, and capacities that can be used to achieve goals.

Level 5: The practitioner communicates regard for the client's feelings, thoughts, potential, and worth as a person and invites the client to identify strengths, resources, and capacities that can be used to achieve goals.

```
1           2           3           4           5
```
Ineffective &/or   Highly Effective &
Inappropriate   Appropriate

<u>Overall Effectiveness of Practitioner Communication</u>
Inappropriate Statements: Minus one point for each statement.   _____

Total Score: Add each point and each circled number to get the total score for the interview.

                                                                                                                _____
                                                                                                                Score

Written Exercise C: Advanced Reflecting Skills

Advanced reflecting responses are reflective comments that identify values, meanings, main themes, and expectations related to the problem (Ivey, 1994). In advanced reflecting, you use everything you know about your client plus your experience, your observations, and your intuition to "go beyond what the client has explicitly expressed to feelings and meanings only implied in the client's statements" (Hammond, Hepworth, & Smith, 1977, p.137). The purpose of advanced reflection or additive empathy, as it is often called, is "to help your clients develop the kind of insight that will lead to problem-managing action" (Egan, 1990, p. 78). Using advanced reflecting skills invites your client to move from focusing on external causes of problems and challenges to focusing on the meaning of the challenges in your client's life (Carkhuff & Anthony, 1979). Before using advanced reflecting, it is important to have a good working relationship with your client and to have a solid understanding of his/her perspective.

Objective of Exercise: To recognize advanced reflecting responses.

Directions: Identify advanced reflecting responses.

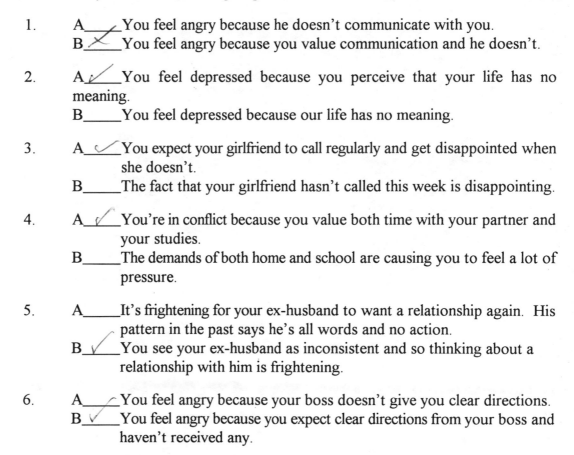

1.   A_____You feel angry because he doesn't communicate with you.
        B__✗__You feel angry because you value communication and he doesn't.

2.   A__✓__You feel depressed because you perceive that your life has no meaning.
        B_____You feel depressed because our life has no meaning.

3.   A__✓__You expect your girlfriend to call regularly and get disappointed when she doesn't.
        B_____The fact that your girlfriend hasn't called this week is disappointing.

4.   A__✓__You're in conflict because you value both time with your partner and your studies.
        B_____The demands of both home and school are causing you to feel a lot of pressure.

5.   A_____It's frightening for your ex-husband to want a relationship again. His pattern in the past says he's all words and no action.
        B__✓__You see your ex-husband as inconsistent and so thinking about a relationship with him is frightening.

6.   A_____You feel angry because your boss doesn't give you clear directions.
        B__✓__You feel angry because you expect clear directions from your boss and haven't received any.

Skill-Building 8: Advanced Reflecting

Objective of Exercise: To practice making advanced reflecting skills in order to identify values, meaning, and expectations related to the problem and to practice communicating empathy. You will be using everything you know about your client and about human nature to hunch or guess about what might be just below the surface of what the client has already said. With these statements, you are moving the focus from things your client has no control over, such as other people's behavior, to things your client can do something about. It is important that you build on the agenda of the client and stay within the client's frame of reference (Cournoyer, 1996).

Directions for Exercise:

1.   Form groups of three people. You will each play the roles of the practitioner, client, and peer supervisor.

2.   Each practitioner/client session will be ten minutes long.

3.   The client will discuss a problem.

4.   The practitioner will communicate involvement, observe, start with a beginning statement, listen carefully, reflect feelings and content, ask questions, and seek clarification.

5.   The practitioner will also make one or more advanced reflecting statements.

6.   During the interview, the peer supervisor will watch the practitioner's use of behaviors that communicate involvement, observe the client, listen to the client, give one point for each item completed on the beginning process list, and keep track of time. In order to evaluate each response, the peer supervisor will write down each response after the beginning statement.

The following activities will be completed after the interview:

7.   The client will share how he/she experienced the practitioner.

8.   The practitioner will evaluate her/his use of advanced reflecting skills. This is a difficult skill and you may find that you have to stop the interview and get help from the peer supervisor, your client, or your instructor in order to create an advanced reflecting response.

9.   The peer supervisor will go over each practitioner responses and give one

54

point for each type of skill used by the practitioner.

10.   The peer supervisor will ask the practitioner to describe what he/she observed and heard from the client and will ask the practitioner to summarize what the client said. The peer supervisor will evaluate the practitioner's use of activities that communicate involvement, the practitioner's ability to accurately observe, the practitioner's active listening skills, beginning process skills, questioning skills, and seeking clarification skills and check for the use of any inappropriate responses. She/he will evaluate how well information about the problems or challenges, the person, and the situation was covered. The peer supervisor will also evaluate the practitioner's use of the core interpersonal qualities of warmth and respect.

11.   With the addition of advanced reflecting, the peer supervisor will use the advanced reflecting evaluation scale.

Advanced Reflecting Skills Evaluation Scale

Level 1:   The practitioner makes very little attempt to verbalize understanding of content, feelings, and meanings.

Level 2:   The practitioner moderately verbalizes understanding of content, feelings, and meanings.

Level 3:   The practitioner consistently verbalizes understanding of content, feelings, but not meanings.

Level 4:   The practitioner generally provides reflections that invite the client to a deeper understanding of his/her behaviors, thoughts, feelings, and interactions with others.

Level 5:   The practitioner appropriately and sensitively able to provide reflections that invite the client to a deeper understanding of her/his behaviors, thoughts, and feelings, and interactions with others.

12.   The peer supervisor will also evaluate the practitioner's use of the core interpersonal quality of empathy.

Empathy Evaluation Scale

Level 1:   The practitioner is not listening. She/he communicates no awareness of the client's expressed feelings and expressions.

Level 2:   The practitioner occasionally responds to the client's expressed feelings.

Level 3:   The practitioner expresses essentially the same feelings, content, and/or meaning as the client.

Level 4:   The practitioner communicates an understanding and acceptance of the validity of the client's point of view.

Level 5:   The practitioner communicates a clear understanding of the client's felt experience and acceptance of the validity of the client's experience. The practitioner verbalizes previously unexpressed feelings and/or meanings.

Practitioners use reflective skills to express their empathic understanding of clients.

13.   Continue until each person has been in each role.

Advanced Reflecting Evaluation Form

Name of Practitioner_____

Name of Peer Supervisor_____

Directions: Under each category (in italics) is a list of behaviors or skills. Give one point for each specific behavior or skill exhibited by the practitioner. On the scales, circle the number that best represents your evaluation of the appropriateness, effectiveness, or completeness of the practitioner's overall use of the skills or behaviors in the category.

Basic Interpersonal Skills

Communicating Involvement: Give one point for each behavior used by the practitioner. Using the scale, circle the number that represents your evaluation of the effectiveness of the practitioner's overall use of behaviors that communicate involvement.

1.	Open and accessible body posture	_____
2.	Congruent facial expression	_____
3.	Slightly inclined toward the client	_____
4.	Directly face the client	_____
4.	Regular eye contact unless inappropriate	_____
5.	No distracting behavior	_____
6.	Minimal encouragement	_____

1	2	3	4	5
Ineffective				Highly Effective

Observing: The practitioner will describe the client. Give one point for each item described accurately. Using the scale, circle the number that best represents your evaluation of the overall completeness of the practitioner's descriptions.

1.	Facial expression	_____
2.	Eye movement and contact	_____
3.	Body position and movement	_____
4.	Breathing patterns	_____
5.	Muscle tone	_____
6.	Gestures	_____
7.	Skin tone changes	_____

1	2	3	4	5
Incomplete				Complete

Active Listening Skills—Content and Process: Using the scale, circle the number that best represents your evaluation of the accuracy and completeness of the practitioner's summary of what the client said and description of the client's way of speaking including speaking style, vocal tone and volume, and speed of delivery.

1	2	3	4	5
Incomplete				Complete

Beginning Process Skills: Give one point for each topic covered by the practitioner. Using the scale, circle the number that best represents your evaluation of the appropriateness and effectiveness of the practitioner's use of beginning skills.

1. Introduce yourself and your role _____
2. Seek introductions _____
3. Identify where meeting will be held _____
4. Identify how long meeting will last _____
5. Describe the initial purpose of the meeting _____
6. Explain some of the things you will do _____
7. Outline the client's role _____
8. Discuss ethical and agency policies _____
9. Seek feedback from the client _____

1	2	3	4	5
Ineffective &/or Inappropriate				Highly Effective & Appropriate

—— Exploring Process

Advanced Reflecting Skills: Give one point for each skill used by the practitioner. Using the scale, circle the number that best represents your evaluation of the appropriateness and effectiveness of the practitioner's use of reflecting skills.

1. Reflecting content _____
2. Reflecting feelings _____
3. Reflecting feeling, content, and/or meaning _____
4. Advanced reflecting _____

With the addition of advanced reflecting, you will be using a more comprehensive evaluation of reflective skills scale.

Advanced Reflecting Skills Evaluation Scale

Level 1: The practitioner makes very little attempt to verbalize understanding of content, feelings, and meanings.

Level 2: The practitioner moderately verbalizes understanding of content, feelings, and meanings.

Level 3: The practitioner consistently verbalizes understanding of content and feelings, but not meanings.

Level 4:   The practitioner generally provides reflections that invite the client to a deeper understanding of his/her behaviors, thoughts, feelings, and interactions with others.

Level 5:   The practitioner appropriately and sensitively able to provide reflections that invite the client to a deeper understanding of her/his behaviors, thoughts, feelings, and interactions with others.

1 _____ 2 _____ 3 _____ 4 _____ 5
Ineffective &/or   Highly Effective &
Inappropriate   Appropriate

Questioning Skills: Give one point for each skill used by the practitioner. Using the scale, circle the number that best represents your evaluation of the appropriateness and effectiveness of the practitioner's use of questioning skills.

1.   Use of open-ended questions   _____
2.   Use of one question at a time   _____
3.   Correct use of closed-ended questions _____

1 _____ 2 _____ 3 _____ 4 _____ 5
Ineffective &/or   Highly Effective &
Inappropriate   Appropriate

Person, Problem/Challenge, and Situation Over Time Exploration: Give one point for each item covered. Using the scale, circle the number that best represents your evaluation of the level of clarity and completeness in each of the three areas.

1.   <u>Problems or Challenges</u>
      Previous attempts to solve problem(s)   _____
      History of the problem(s)   _____
      Precipitating factors   _____
      Severity or intensity of the problem(s) _____

1 _____ 2 _____ 3 _____ 4 _____ 5
No Information   Complete Information

2.   <u>Person</u>
      Feelings about having the problem(s)   _____
      Effect of the problem(s) on functioning _____
      Personal strengths   _____

1 _____ 2 _____ 3 _____ 4 _____ 5
No Information   Complete Information

3.   Situation
        Effect of the problem(s) on others   _____
        Available social support   _____
        Demands and stresses in the situation/environment _____
        Strengths in the situation/environment   _____

1	2	3	4	5
No Information				Complete Information

Seeking Clarification Give one point for each skill used by the practitioner. Using the scale, circle the number that represents your evaluation of the appropriateness and effectiveness of the practitioner's use of seeking clarification skills.

1.   Exploring the meaning of words and body language   _____
2.   Exploring the basis of conclusions drawn by the client   _____
3.   Exploring statements that appear contradictory   _____
4.   Exploring details regarding interaction   _____

1	2	3	4	5
Ineffective &/or Inappropriate				Highly Effective & Appropriate

Core Interpersonal Qualities

Using the scale, circle the number that best represents you evaluation of the evaluate the appropriateness and effectiveness of the practitioner's use of warmth, respect, and empathy.

Warmth   _____
Respect   _____

1	2	3	4	5
Ineffective &/or Inappropriate				Highly Effective & Appropriate

Empathy Evaluation Scale

Level 1:   The practitioner is not listening. She/he communicates no awareness of the client's expressed feelings and expressions.

Level 2:   The practitioner occasionally responds to the client's expressed feelings.

Level 3:   The practitioner expresses essentially the same feelings, content and/or meaning as the client.

Level 4:   The practitioner communicates an understanding and acceptance of the validity of the client's point of view.

Level 5:   The practitioner communicates a clear understanding of the client's felt experience and acceptance of the validity of the client's experience. The practitioner verbalizes previously unexpressed feelings and/or meanings.

1	2	3	4	5
Ineffective &/or Inappropriate				Highly Effective & Appropriate

<u>Overall Effectiveness of Practitioner Communication</u>
Inappropriate Statements: Minus one point for each statement　　　_____

Total Score:　Add each point and each circled number to get the total score for the interview.

$$_____$$
Score

Communication Scale

Objective of Scale: To give abbreviated names for the types of responses you have studied.

Inappropriate ways of communicating with clients (IN)
Beginning process statements (BP)
Using minimal encouragement (ME)
Reflecting content (RC)
Reflecting feelings (RF)
Reflecting feeling and content (RFC)
Asking closed-ended questions (CQ)
Asking open-ended questions (OQ)
Seeking clarification (SC)
Advanced Reflection (AR)

Examples of each type of response

If your client says, "I never seem to be able to get to work on time." Here are possible responses and the name of the response.

Inappropriate (IN)
"Well, that happens to me too," or
"Have you tried buying an alarm clock?"

Reflecting content (RC)
"You are often late for work," or
"You are having trouble getting to work on time."

Reflecting feeling (RF)
"It sounds like you are feeling frustrated," or
"You sound troubled."

Reflecting feeling and content (RFC)
"You sound troubled about the fact that you are so often late to work," or
"Being late to work is frustrating to you."

Close-ended question (CQ)
"When did this last happen?" or
"Is your job in jeopardy?"

Open-ended question (OQ)
"Can you tell me more about this situation?" or
"What is it like for you to be late?"

Seeking clarification (SC)
"Are you saying that you are late every day?" or "About how late do you get to work?"

Advanced reflecting (AR)

"You feel guilty about being late so often because you value doing well," or
"You feel frustrated with yourself because you expect yourself to be more self-disciplined and get up on time."

Written Exercise D: Naming Statements Using the Communication Scale

Directions: The purpose of this exercise is to practice naming responses. Below the client's statement are possible responses. Rate each response using the Communication Scale.

1. <u>Husband speaking to wife</u>: "I think I'm going to quit. George is on my back again. He just nit picks. Everything has to be just perfect! He ought to sit where I sit for a day and see what it's like to have a thousand interruptions while you're trying to fill out those dumb forms."
   Wife responding:
   _____ a.   "That would be a fine thing for you to do in our financial state!"
   _____ b.   "You're really upset."
   _____ c.   "Must have been a terrible day."
   _____ d.   "You're furious because George doesn't understand how hard it is to fulfill his demands."

2. <u>Wife speaking to husband</u>: "Nobody appreciates me around here. I work my tail off trying to keep the house neat, the clothes clean, and making good meals. What do I get in return? Kids who fight with each other and a husband who sits and stares at the TV. Sometimes I really wonder if it's worth it."
   Husband responding:
   _____ a.   "Boy, you're sure down this evening."
   _____ b.   "You make me sick - you've got life so easy, no boss, no pressures, no nothing and here you are feeling sorry for yourself!"
   _____ c.   "The lack of appreciation you're getting from the kids and me has you really low."
   _____ d.   "Sometimes it seems nobody cares."

3. <u>Ten-year-old girl speaking to parents</u>: "I don't see why I can't go to the slumber party. Sally and Patty get to go. You won't let me do anything like the other kids." (Hits her fist on the arm of the chair.)
   Parent responding:
   _____ a.   "You're furious with me because I won't let you go!"
   _____ b.   "Why don't you invite Jennifer over here for the evening."
   _____ c.   "That's the way it is and I don't want to hear about it anymore."
   _____ d.   "Sometimes you feel pretty cheated because I won't let you do what other kids do."

4. <u>Friend to friend</u>: "Did I ever have a neat day today! My supervisor gave me a copy of my evaluation and it was really complimentary. She's going to recommend me for a promotion."

Friend responding:

_____ a.   "Wish my day had been like that. I had a real bummer."

_____ b.   "Some people have all the luck."

_____ c.   "Sounds like you are feeling terrific and rewarded for your hard work."

_____ d.   "You're really high."

5. <u>Five year old to parent</u>: "I wish I could stay home. I don't want to go to kindergarten tomorrow. What do you think the children will be like? What do you think my teacher will be like? Maybe they won't like me."

Parent responding:

_____ a.   "You're kind of scared about having to meet your new teacher and the other kids because you are not sure they will like you."

_____ b.   "You don't want to be a dummy do you? You have to go to school so you can learn."

_____ c.   "You are five years old now and I want you to act like it. I don't want any bad reports from the teacher."

_____ d.   "I'll be glad to walk you to your room tomorrow."

6. <u>Client to practitioner</u>: "I'm calling to see if you could help me. I just found out that I'm ten weeks pregnant and I don't know what to do. I don't know whether to get an abortion or place the baby for adoption. Abortion would be faster, but I'm not sure that I believe in it."

Practitioner responding:

_____ a.   "You see both the positive and the negative in abortion."

_____ b.   "You sound really confused because one part of you wants to have an abortion but another part of you questions that."

_____ c.   "Having to choose between the two has you really mixed up."

_____ d.   "You sound troubled and confused."

7. <u>Client to practitioner</u>: I just stopped by to see if you had any leads on jobs. I've been job-hunting for six months now with no results. I'm getting so tired that I don't even care anymore. I'm beginning to wonder if I'll ever work again!"

Practitioner responding:

_____ a.   "You've been looking a long time."

_____ b.   "I've just been through the same thing myself but finally lucked out and got this job."

_____ c.   "You sound really discouraged because the job market seems so bad."

_____ d.   "Things will get better, they have to."

IV

CONTRACTING PROCESS

After fully exploring the problem, person, and situation, the practitioner needs to help clients identify the problems or challenges to work on and their goals. In this section, you will be focusing on: Reaching Agreement about Problems and Challenges, Reaching Agreement about Goals, and Reaching Agreement about Specific Goals and Establishing a Contract for Work. With these responses, clients are invited to think about aspects of their thinking, feeling, and acting that they are uncomfortable with and want to change. Reading this chapter will give you an overview of the skills you will be learning.

The first step in contracting is reaching agreement about the problems that you will be working on. It is important for the practitioner to state or restate the problems or challenges to be sure there is clear understanding between the practitioner and the client. Often, this response will involve partializing, or breaking a complex problem/situation into more manageable parts. As you know from your own life, big problems can seem overwhelming, but when you divide the larger problem into parts it seems easier to handle. For example, if your problem is that you don't have enough money to pay your bills and you feel scared, you might break the problem down into several parts such as: you are unemployed, your apartment is too expensive, you are spending too much money on books, and so on. Each of the separate problems probably seem more manageable than the large problem.

The next step in contracting is reaching agreement about goals. "Final goals are the envisioned aims toward which cognitive, emotional, behavioral, and situational actions are directed" (Cournoyer, 1996, p. 256). These goals should be mutually established between you and your clients. You will use your questioning skills and seeking clarification skills to help your clients figure out what goals they are motivated to achieve. Cournoyer suggests asking, "How will you know when a particular problem is resolved?" (1996, p. 257) The solution-focused approach would suggest asking clients to describe what their life would be

like if a miracle happened and their problems were solved (de Shazer, 1985; Furman & Ahola, 1992; O'Hanlon & Weiner-Davis, 1989; Walter & Peller, 1992). Many practitioners use final or end point goals and also process goals. As you work with your client to figure out what steps are necessary to reach your final goal, you are creating a map or plan for your work together. Each of these steps can be identified as process goals or goals that lead to the achievement of the final goal.

From general goals, the practitioner will work with the client to establish agreed-upon **m**easurable, **a**ttainable, **p**ositive, **s**pecific (MAPS) goals. As we know, with clear MAPS goals, we are much more likely to get where we are going. Also, the plan for evaluating goal achievement will be more effective when the goals meet the MAPS criterion.

The final aspect of the contracting process is the establishment of a plan that identifies the roles and expectations of the client and practitioner. This plan should include how often you will meet with your client and how many appointments you will have before evaluating.

General Form of Communication from Reflecting through Reaching Agreement about Goals

Reflecting feeling and content
You feel _____ because she/he/it/they _____.

Advanced reflection
You feel _____ because you think _____.
- you expect
- you hope or wish for
- you imagine

Reaching agreement about the problems or challenges.
You feel _____ because you have not been able to _____.
- get organized
- control your anger
- decide what to do about an abusive situation
- stop drinking

Reaching agreement about the goals.
You want to be able to _____.

- schedule your time better
- express your anger appropriately
- keep yourself safe
- be sober

Reaching agreement about specific goals
Your goal is _____.

- to use one hour per day for the next month to organize your house
- to pay attention to your feelings, notice when you begin to feel angry, and take five minutes to consider you options before expressing your anger
- within two days to create a plan with your neighbor and your children that will allow you to get out of the house anytime you notice that your husband has been drinking and to attend the women's support group in order to decide whether to stay in this relationship
- to attend AA meetings everyday for thirty days, get a sponsor, and talk to your sponsor immediately any time you want to drink

Complete Communication Scale

Objective of Scale: To give abbreviated names for the types of responses you have studied.

Inappropriate ways of communicating with clients	(IN)
Beginning process statements	(BP)
Using minimal encouragement	(ME)
Reflecting content	(RC)
Reflecting feelings	(RF)
Reflecting feeling and content	(RFC)
Asking closed-ended questions	(CQ)
Asking open-ended questions	(OQ)
Seeking clarification	(SC)
Advanced reflection	(AR)
Reaching agreement about the problems or challenges	(AP)
Reaching agreement about the goals	(AG)
Defining the goals (MAPS)	(DG)
Establishing the contract	(EC)

Examples of Contracting Responses

Reaching agreement about the problems or challenges   (AP)

    Your feelings of sadness and lack of energy have made it difficult for you to pay attention to your children.

    Your anxiety about getting all the work done has made you irritable with your employees.

Reaching agreement about the goals   (AG)

    You want to be aware of the needs of your children.

    You want to be more responsive to the needs of your employees.

Defining the goals (MAPS)   (DG)

    Your goal is to allow at least fifteen minutes every day to focus all your attention on your children.

    Your goal is to set aside thirty minutes each day when you will be available to talk to your employees.

Establishing the contract   (EC)

    Our agreement is to meet weekly for fifty minutes to resolve issues that may be making it hard for you to focus your attention on your children. In our sixth appointment, we will evaluate whether you have achieved your goal. If necessary, we will discuss contracting for more appointments.

    Our agreement is to meet weekly for fifty minutes to resolve issues that may be making it hard for you to set aside thirty minutes each day in order to be available to talk to your employees. In our fourth appointment, we will evaluate whether you have achieved your goal. If necessary, we will discuss contracting for more appointments.

Example: Naming a Series of Transactions

Directions: In order to become familiar with the Communication Scale, read each communication and analyze the reasons for each rating score.

    <u>Client</u>:   "I'm so upset today that I can't even think. Last night my husband went to the bars and never came home. He's been dry for about a year and now he's starting over again."

    <u>Practitioner</u>:   "You're really angry because he's started drinking again." (RFC)

Client: "Yes, I'm angry and hurt, too. Really hurt. I've given up all kinds of things I'm interested in to be home and be with him to help keep him dry and then he goes and does this."

Practitioner: "You feel bitter because you've sacrificed to help him and this is your thanks." (RFC)

Client: "Right. I've been working so hard to make our life together enjoyable so he would not want to go out and drink."

Practitioner: "You feel resentful because you have put so much effort into the relationship and he is still drinking." (RFC)

Client: "I had made a life for myself without him because he drank so much, but when he said he wanted my help, I agreed. I have kept my end of the deal."

Practitioner: "You feel betrayed because he asked for your help and then didn't use it." (RFC)

Client: "He sure didn't. I've been told all alcoholics are con-artists and now I believe it."

Practitioner: "You feel angry because he conned you into believing he really would change. (RFC)

Client: "I sure feel conned. He seemed so sincere and so willing to be different. He even cried."

Practitioner: "You feel confused because his behavior was so convincing and yet he didn't keep his promise." (RFC)

Client: "I am really confused. If I had behaved like he did, I would mean it."

Practitioner: "You feel bewildered because you expect people to follow through on promises and your husband didn't." (AR)

Client: "Yes, that's what I expect. I had gone out of my way to help him."

Practitioner: "You feel hurt because you expect people to take your help and use it when you give it." (AR)

Client:	"Yes, that is my expectation. I was awful to him this morning. I berated him terribly. I was so angry I just couldn't stop myself from yelling."
Practitioner:	"You feel discouraged because you have not been able to stop yourself from berating him after he's been drinking." (AP)
Client:	"It's really hard for me to stop, but I don't want to act that way."
Practitioner:	"You want to be able to restrain from attacking or berating him." (AG)

Example: Personal Problems and Challenges

You have not been able to:
    assert yourself when your rights are being violated
    listen to others without interrupting
    respond to others' feelings
    state your preference and ask for what you want
    stop working so much
    move out of the house
    stop being a referee for your children
    stop rebelling
    stop giving so much to others
    let go of your child
    give your spouse space
    be firm with your child
    be consistent with your child regarding rules
    stop yourself from drinking, eating, smoking, or going out compulsively
    let others help you out
    stop yourself from making condescending remarks, criticizing, or verbally attacking
        others
    manage your money
    stop yourself from physically hurting your wife or your children
    stop talking about physical ailments
    stop yelling and calling names when you argue
    make yourself get to work on time
    stop blaming others
    stop yourself from controlling and manipulating others
    nurture yourself or others
    discipline yourself

trust men/women/people
respond appropriately to anger
respond to put-downs
accept compliments
say "no" and stay with it
stop telling yourself that others should do what you want them to do
stop telling yourself that you are a failure
stop telling yourself that you should be able to please your children
stop telling yourself that something bad is going to happen to you
stop telling yourself that you deserve to be punished
stop telling yourself that there is a right and perfect solution that must be found
stop telling yourself that you don't have a right to exist

Written Exercise E: Recognizing Responses that Reach Agreement about Problems and Challenges

Objective of Exercise: To learn to recognize responses that identify the problems or challenges

Directions: Check the response that identifies the client's problem or challenge.
<u>Hint</u>: You can only solve problems that belong to you. You can't make another person change.

1. A____You feel discouraged because you can't get your husband to stop smoking.
    B____Your inability to stop telling your husband that smoking is bad for him has you discouraged.

2. A____The way you see your boss managing the business is frustrating to you and you wish he'd get organized.
    B____Your inability to make recommendations to your boss is frustrating to you.

3. A____When being asked for money from your friend, you are not happy with your inability to say "no."
    B____You feel put upon because you think your friend is using you.

4. A ____You are upset because your lack of initiative keeps you from applying for a job you're qualified for.
    B____You're upset because you believe you could have that better job and you wish you had the initiative.

5. A____You cannot believe people really feel like you do.
    B____You're unable to determine if people feel like you do or not since you're not able to tell them how you feel.

6. A____I wish you would spend more time with me.
    B____I haven't found a way to invite you to want to be with me.

7. A____I am frustrated because I haven't been able to motivate you to do excellent work.
    B____I value excellent work.

Skill-Building 9: Reaching Agreement about Problem(s) and Challenge(s)

Objective of Exercise: To practice making responses that reach for agreement about problems or challenges and to practice communicating in a genuine way.

Directions for Exercise:

1. Form groups of three people. You will each play the roles of the practitioner, client, and peer supervisor.

2. Each practitioner/client session will be fifteen minutes long.

3. The client will discuss a problem.

4. The practitioner will communicate involvement, observe, listen carefully, start with a beginning statement, ask questions, seek clarification, and use reflecting responses.

5. The practitioner will also make responses that identify the client's problems or challenges. If you are not able to make a response that reaches agreement about problems or challenges in the interview, stop ask for help from your peer supervisor, your client, or your instructor.

6. During the interview, the peer supervisor will watch the practitioner's use of behaviors that communicate involvement, observe the client, listen to the client, will give one point for each item completed on the beginning process list, and keep track of time. In order to evaluate each response, the peer supervisor will write down each response after the beginning statement.

The following activities will be completed after the interview:

7. The client will share how he/she experienced the practitioner.

8. The practitioner will evaluate her/his use of responses that reach agreement about the problem(s) or challenge(s).

9. The peer supervisor will go over each response and give one point for each type of skill used by the practitioner.

10. The peer supervisor will ask the practitioner to describe what she/he observed and heard from the client and will ask the practitioner to summarize what the client said. The peer supervisor will evaluate the practitioner's use

of activities that communicate involvement, the practitioner's ability to accurately observe, the practitioner's active listening skills, beginning process skills, reflecting skills, questioning skills, and seeking clarification skills and will will check for any use of inappropriate responses. She/he will evaluate how well information about problem(s) or challenge(s), person, and situation was covered. The peer supervisor will also evaluate the practitioner's use of the core interpersonal qualities of warmth, respect, and empathy.

11. The peer supervisor will give one point for each responses that reachs for agreement about the problem(s) or challenge(s).

12. The peer supervisor will also evaluate the practitioner's use of the core interpersonal quality of genuineness.

Genuineness Evaluation Scale

Level 1: The practitioner's words are clearly unrelated to his/her present feelings.

Level 2: His/her words seem to be only slightly related to his/her present feelings. He/ she appears sincere some of the time.

Level 3: The counselor appears moderately sincere but not fully present.

Level 4: The practitioner generally appears sincere and fully present and sometimes shares his/her reactions with the client.

Level 5: The practitioner appears completely sincere, fully present, and able to appropriately use and share reactions with the client.

13. Continue until each person has been in each role.

Agreement about Problems Evaluation Form

Name of Practitioner_____

Name of Peer Supervisor_____

Directions: Under each category (in italics) is a list of behaviors or skills. Give one point for each specific behavior or skill exhibited by the practitioner. On the scales, circle the number that best represents your evaluation of the appropriateness, effectiveness, or completeness of the practitioner's overall use of the skills or behaviors in the category.

Basic Interpersonal Skills

Communicating Involvement: Give one point for each behavior used by the practitioner. Using the scale, circle the number that represents your evaluation of the effectiveness of the practitioner's overall use of behaviors that communicate involvement.

1. Open and accessible body posture _____
2. Congruent facial expression _____
3. Slightly inclined toward the client _____
4. Directly face the client _____
4. Regular eye contact unless inappropriate _____
5. No distracting behavior _____
6. Minimal encouragement _____

1	2	3	4	5
Ineffective				Highly Effective

Observing: The practitioner will describe the client. Give one point for each item described accurately. Using the scale, circle the number that best represents your evaluation of the overall completeness of the practitioner's descriptions.

1. Facial expression _____
2. Eye movement and contact _____
3. Body position and movement _____
4. Breathing patterns _____
5. Muscle tone _____
6. Gestures _____
7. Skin tone changes _____

1	2	3	4	5
Incomplete				Complete

Active Listening Skills—Content and Process: Using the scale, circle the number that best represents your evaluation of the accuracy and completeness of the practitioner's summary of what the client said and description of the client's way of speaking including speaking style, vocal tone and volume, and speed of delivery.

1	2	3	4	5
Incomplete				Complete

Beginning Process Skills: Give one point for each topic covered by the practitioner. Using the scale, circle the number that best represents your evaluation of the appropriateness and effectiveness of the practitioner's use of beginning skills.

1. Introduce yourself and your role _____
2. Seek introductions _____
3. Identify where meeting will be held _____
4. Identify how long meeting will last _____
5. Describe the initial purpose of the meeting _____
6. Explain some of the things you will do _____
7. Outline the client's role _____
8. Discuss ethical and agency policies _____
9. Seek feedback from the client _____

1	2	3	4	5
Ineffective &/or Inappropriate				Highly Effective & Appropriate

Exploring Process

Advanced Reflecting Skills: Give one point for each skill used by the practitioner. Using the scale, circle the number that best represents your evaluation of the appropriateness and effectiveness of the practitioner's use of reflecting skills.

1. Reflecting content _____
2. Reflecting feelings _____
3. Reflecting feeling, content, and/or meaning _____
4. Advanced reflecting _____

1	2	3	4	5
Ineffective &/or Inappropriate				Highly Effective & Appropriate

Questioning Skills: Give one point for each skill used by the practitioner. Using the scale, circle the number that best represents your evaluation of the appropriateness and effectiveness of the practitioner's use of questioning skills.

1. Use of open-ended questions _____
2. Use of one question at a time _____
3. Correct use of closed-ended questions _____

1	2	3	4	5
Ineffective &/or Inappropriate				Highly Effective & Appropriate

Person, Problem/Challenge, and Situation Over Time Exploration: Give one point for each item covered. Using the scale, circle the number that best represents your evaluation of the level of clarity and completeness in each of the three areas.

1.   <u>Problems or Challenges</u>
       Previous attempts to solve problem(s)   _____
       History of the problem(s)   _____
       Precipitating factors   _____
       Severity or intensity of the problem(s)   _____

1	2	3	4	5
No Information				Complete Information

2.   <u>Person</u>
       Feelings about having the problem(s)   _____
       Effect of the problem(s) on functioning   _____
       Personal strengths   _____

1	2	3	4	5
No Information				Complete Information

3.   <u>Situation</u>
       Effect of the problem(s) on others   _____
       Available social support   _____
       Demands and stresses in the situation/environment   _____
       Strengths in the situation/environment   _____

1	2	3	4	5
No Information				Complete Information

Seeking Clarification: Give one point for each skill used by the practitioner. Using the scale, circle the number that represents your evaluation of the appropriateness and effectiveness of the practitioner's use of seeking clarification skills.

1.   Exploring the meaning of words and body language   _____
2.   Exploring the basis of conclusions drawn by the client   _____
3.   Exploring statements that appear contradictory   _____
4.   Exploring details regarding interaction   _____

1	2	3	4	5
Ineffective &/or Inappropriate				Highly Effective & Appropriate

<u>Contracting Process</u>
Skills Related to Reaching Agreement about Problems or Challenges and Goals: Give one point if this skill was used by the practitioner.

1.   Reaching agreement about problem(s) or challenges   _____

Core Interpersonal Qualities

Using the scale, determine the number that best represents your evaluation of the appropriateness and effectiveness of the practitioner's expression of each quality. Write your evaluation number on the line following each quality.

Warmth _____

Respect _____

Empathy _____

1	2	3	4	5

Ineffective &/or   Highly Effective &
Inappropriate   Appropriate

Genuineness Evaluation Scale

Level 1:   The practitioner's words are clearly unrelated to his/her present feelings.

Level 2:   His/her words seem to be only slightly related to his/her present feelings. He/she appears sincere some of the time.

Level 3:   The counselor appears moderately sincere but not fully present.

Level 4:   The practitioner generally appears sincere and fully present and sometimes shares his/her reactions with the client.

Level 5:   The practitioner appears completely sincere, fully present and able to appropriately use and share reactions with the client.

1	2	3	4	5

Ineffective &/or   Highly Effective &
Inappropriate   Appropriate

Overall Effectiveness of Practitioner Communication

Inappropriate Statements: Minus one point for each inappropriate statement. ____

Total Score: Add each point and each circled or written number to get a total score for the interview.

_____
Score

Written Exercise F: Recognizing Responses that Reach Agreement about Goals

Objective of Exercise: To be able to recognize goal statements.

Directions: In this exercise, there is a problem identifying communication. Below this communication are two possible responses. Identify the response that reaches agreement about goals. Your homework should be completed before doing the in-class exercise on reaching agreement about goals.

1. The fact that you can't say "no" to your daughter when she asks for help is discouraging to you.
   _____You want to be able to say "no" to your daughter when she asks for your help.
   _____You wish your daughter would become more independent.

2. Your inability to share personal problems without crying is depressing to you.
   _____You want your problems to be less intense so you won't cry.
   _____Being able to share personal problems without crying is important to you.

3. Not managing to complete one household task before starting another is frustrating to you.
   _____You wish your household tasks would get done.
   _____It's important to you to change your pattern of doing household tasks so that you complete one before starting another.

4. Getting low ratings from your supervisor is worrying you.
   _____You'd like your supervisor to give you higher ratings.
   _____You plan to develop a plan with your supervisor for raising your ratings.

5. Not getting a raise is depressing to you.
   _____You are going to discuss this problem with your supervisor.
   _____Your goal is to get your supervisor to give you a raise.

6. You can't stop complaining about your husband's drinking.
   _____Your goal is to get your husband to stop drinking
   _____You plan to stop talking to your husband about his drinking.

80

Written Exercise G: Naming Responses Using the Communication Scale

Objective of Exercise: To practice naming responses using the Communication Scale.

Directions: Identify each of the numbered responses using the Communication Scale. Your homework should be completed before doing the in-class exercise on reaching agreement about goals.

Teacher and Mother of Student:

(Teacher) "I asked you to come in today because I'm having some difficulty with your son in the classroom. I didn't have any problems with him at the beginning of the year but recently he has been very difficult. He can't sit still."

(Mother) "Yes, I know. He's the same way at home. He's been driving me crazy. He messes around so much getting ready for school that I have to yell at him or he'd be late. By the time the bus comes, I'm a nervous wreck."

1.____(teacher) "His distract ability in the mornings is really upsetting you."

(mother) "Is it ever! The mornings are nothing compared to after school. He comes home from school and fights constantly with his little brother. He can't settle down to anything constructive."

2.____(teacher) "Sounds as though you're really discouraged because he's not really controllable any of the time."

(mother) "Yes, and now to hear you say that he's acting up at school, too, really blows my mind. I just don't know what to do. I've got enough troubles without him acting up. My husband and I are not getting along. We're fighting all of the time, too." (She starts to cry.)

3.____(teacher) "You're feeling pretty down because things aren't going well in your marriage, either."

(mother) "Yes, and now that I am telling you this I'm wondering if maybe my son's behavior is because of all the fighting my husband and I are doing. I know that I'm not giving him very much because I'm so upset with my husband all of the time. I don't know what to do."

4.____(teacher) "You're worried because you see there may be a connection between your son's behavior and your problems with your husband, but you don't know how you can give your son more attention when you are so upset with your husband all of the time."

(mother) "Right. I guess I need someone to talk to about my husband so I can get some of that off my chest. Maybe then I could be more responsive to my son."

Counselor and Stepmother of a Fifteen-Year-Old Son:

(Stepmother) "I'm really worried, my husband leaves for three months on business starting Monday and I don't know what I'm going to do with Robert. He's so hateful to me. Would you believe this, I was scrubbing the kitchen floor on my hands and knees the other day and he came out to the kitchen and dropped nutshells right on the floor in front of me! I'm getting sick just thinking about the next three months."

5.____(practitioner) "You sound somewhat panicky because your husband's leaving you with the full responsibility of Robert."

(stepmother) "Yes, I am. I don't get any support from his grandparents either. In fact, they are against me. Robert goes over to their house and cries about how I treat him and they call my husband and complain."

6.____(practitioner) "You resent the way Robert is manipulating the situation."

(stepmother) "He infuriates me. I get along fine with the other kids, but not Robert. People tell me to just hold on until he goes to college, but I can't possibly stand this for three more years."

7.____(practitioner) "The pressure from all sides is about to cause you to explode."

(stepmother) "Oh, yes. I've got no one to talk to and the pressure just builds and builds. I know I am being crabby to everyone and I don't want to be that way, but I can't help it."

8.____(practitioner) "Your frustration with Robert is affecting your relationships with the rest of the family."

(stepmother) "Yes, I even wake up sick to my stomach in the morning just thinking about dealing with Robert for another day. He hates me, he really does. At least, I think he does. My husband tells me that I just wait for him to do something to prove that he hates me, that I seem to need him to hate me. I don't know, maybe I do, maybe he's right."

9.____(practitioner) "You're really confused right now."

(stepmother) "Yes, I guess I'm beginning to doubt myself."

10.____(practitioner) "Your doubts about yourself make it hard for you to figure out what is going on with Robert."

Parent and Teenager:

Teen: "I wish I didn't have to go to school tomorrow."

11.____(parent) "You seem kind of down this evening."

(teen) "Yeah, I have a test in history tomorrow and I'm not ready for it."

12.____(parent) "Sounds as if the fact that you aren't ready for it has you a little scared."

(teen) "I guess I am. I want to do well, but I don't think I'm going to."

13.____(parent) "You're worried because it's not clicking for you."

(teen) "That's right. I sit here and look at this book and nothing is happening in my head. I hate history!"

14.____"You wish you didn't have to take the test."

(teen) "Right."

15.____(parent) "When you try and you still can't get it, you really get discouraged."

(teen) "That's for sure. If I was messing around, that would be one thing, but I'm not and I still can't get this stuff."

16.____(parent) "It's aggravating to you because you can't figure out what's wrong with your study habits."

(teen) "I guess that's it. I must be going at it all wrong."

17.____"And you'd like to figure out a better way to master history."

(teen) "Yeah, I'm not stupid. I oughta be able to get this stuff."

Client Whose Husband Doesn't Pay Attention to Her

(Client) "I'm sure dreading tonight. We are invited to a party and my husband acts so awful at parties."

18.____(practitioner) "You feel worried because you know his usual way of behaving at such things."

(client) "Yes, he drinks too much and then he starts flirting with all the women."

19.____"You feel jealous because he ignores you."

(client) "Right. I might as well be a hole in the wall for all he knows when he gets going."

20.____(practitioner) "You feel resentful because he acts like you don't exist."

(client) "He really goes for the pretty young ones."

21.____(practitioner) "You feel depressed because he doesn't look at you when there are younger women around."

(client) "Uh-huh. I could just get sick the way he plays up to them."

22.____(practitioner) "You feel disgusted because he really acts differently around them than he does around you."

(client) "If he would at least ask me to dance once in a while, I'd feel better about going to parties with him."

23.____(practitioner) "You feel hurt because you aren't a part of his thoughts when he goes to a party."

(client) "Yes. I wish I could go and have a good time in spite of him, but it's not that easy for a woman to go up and ask a man to dance."

24.____(practitioner) "You feel uncomfortable because you can't assert yourself with men."

(client) "I guess that is what it comes down to because I know there are men who like to be asked by a woman."

25.____(practitioner) "You'd really like to be able to assert yourself and ask men to dance with you."

(client) "Would I ever!"

Overweight Client

(Client) "I have been putting on weight the last few weeks and I just can't stop gaining."

26.____(practitioner) "You are upset because of the jump in your weight."

(client) "Yes, I don't know what to do. I've tried exercising but that doesn't help.

27.____(practitioner) "You feel frustrated because you have tried exercise and it didn't work."

(client) "Yes, and my friends and husband don't help matters. They keep offering fattening foods to me and telling me to eat them"

28.____(practitioner) "You feel angry because other people around you won't help you try to lose weight."

(client) "Right! They know I'm on a diet, but they try to get me to go off of it."

29.____(practitioner) "You feel let down because no one will support you in this effort."

(client) "If they were real friends they would know I'm serious about this and help me stick with it."

30.____(practitioner) "You feel annoyed with your friends because they don't realize that this is important to you."

(client) "Not only that they buy my favorite foods and sit down in front of me and try to entice me into eating them. It is so hard not to. Sometimes I do eat them and they laugh and I feel awful."

31.____(practitioner) "You feel distressed because your friends are so insensitive."

(client) "I just don't know what to do!"

32.____ (practitioner) "You feel discouraged because you expected to lose weight."

(client) "Yes, I thought I would have lost the weight I had gained by now."

33.____(practitioner) "You feel dissatisfied because you wanted to be back to a desirable weight by now."

(client) "Right now I am just as fat as ever."

34.____(practitioner) "You feel weak because you cannot stick to a regimen to lose weight."

(client) "I guess that's it."

35.____(practitioner) "You want to find an effective way to lose weight."

Client Who Can't Concentrate

(client) "I can't seem to get anything done at work anymore, it just seems like the harder I try, the more I fail."

36.____(practitioner) "You feel discouraged because you try and still can't get the job done."

(client) "Yes, I can't seem to concentrate on a task for more than a few minutes. Then I start another task."

37.____(practitioner) "It sounds like you tend to jump from one task to the next."

(client) "Yes and it seems like more and more work piles up until I don't know where to begin. There is so much!"

38.____(practitioner) "You feel dismayed by the amount of work that you have to complete."

(client) "Yes, it's very frightening to think that there seems to be so much work and so little time."

39.____(practitioner) "You feel scared because you are getting so far behind."

(client) "Yes, I feel that my boss expects me to be superwoman. It's not fair."

40.____(practitioner) "You feel cheated because your boss wants so much from you in such a short time."

(client) "I don't understand if I'm just too scatterbrained or if she just expects too much."

41.___(practitioner) "You feel confused about whether you are capable of handling the job or if your boss is just insensitive."

(client) "Yes, I just feel like I'm too confused to figure out the difference."

42.___ (practitioner) "You feel overwhelmed, but you want to be a more productive employee."

(client) "Yes, and I don't know how to do it."

43.___(practitioner) "You feel frustrated because you expect to know how to and yet don't."

(client) "Yes, maybe I just try to get too much done. But I end up getting just a little of each task done."

44.___(practitioner) "You feel mixed."

(client) "Yes, maybe I should know how to set priorities."

45.___(practitioner) "You feel upset with yourself because you are unable to decide where to focus your efforts."

(client) "Maybe things would work out better if I just put all my work away until the task I'm working on is completed."

46.___(practitioner) "You feel upset because you haven't set priorities and you want to make goals for yourself."

Unappreciated Client

(client) "They don't care if you work your butt off here. It seems the more you do, the more they want."

47.___(practitioner) "You feel angry because they push for more all the time at work."

(client) "That's right! I give 100 percent everyday and what thanks do I get? None."

48.___(practitioner) "You feel disgusted because you are working hard and getting little recognition."

(client) "Take the foremen, they treat you as though you're some kind of child. They act like they have to lead you by the hand."

49.___(practitioner) "You feel down-graded by the way the foremen treat everyone."

(client) "And sometimes they'll chew your butt for no apparent reason. That's probably to scare you to into being get more productive."

50.___(practitioner) "You feel irritated because of the tactics they use to get more productive."

(client) "That's right, and I don't have anyone to turn to for help. The union is in with the company."

51.___(practitioner) "You feel depressed because there's no help."

(client) "I was once a working part of the union but the union officials didn't help me. We've got new people in now."

52.___(practitioner) "You feel hurt because of the way the union conducted things or the way the officials did things."

(client) "That sounds about right. And if they did help you, they acted in the same capacity as the foremen. They treated you like some kind of kid."

53.___(practitioner) "You feel hurt because of the way you are treated by the union."

(client) "It takes good people to make a functioning union. I've tried to get people involved, but they just won't help."

54.___(practitioner) "You feel discouraged because you can't get people involved to make a good union."

(client) "The union is only as good as the people."

55.___(practitioner) "You want to be able to organize the people.

Skill-Building 10: Reaching Agreement about Goals

Objective of Exercise: To practice making responses that identify the problems or challenges and the goals.

Directions for Exercise:

1. Form groups of three people. You will each play the roles of the practitioner, client, and peer supervisor.

2. Each practitioner/client session will be fifteen minutes long.

3. The client will discuss a problem.

4. The practitioner will communicate involvement, observe, start with a beginning statement, listen carefully, ask questions, seek clarification, reflect, and make responses that reach for agreement about problems or challenges.

5. The practitioner will also make responses that reach for agreement about goals. If you need to stop the interview and figure out your response or ask for help, that is okay.

6. During the interview, the peer supervisor will watch the practitioner's use of behaviors that communicate involvement, observe the client, listen to the client, give one point for each item completed on the beginning process list, and keep track of time. In order to evaluate each response, the peer supervisor will write down each response after the beginning statement.

The following activities will be completed after the interview:

7. The client will share how he/she experienced the practitioner.

8. The practitioner will evaluate her/his use of responses that reach for agreement about the goals.

9. The peer supervisor will go over each response and check each type of skill used by the practitioner.

10. The peer supervisor will ask the practitioner to describe what he/she observed and heard from the client, will ask the practitioner to summarize what the client said. The peer supervisor will evaluate the practitioner's

use of activities that communicate involvement, the practitioner's ability to accurately observe, the practitioner's active listening skills, beginning process skills, reflecting skills, questioning skills, seeking clarification skills and will give a minus point for any use of inappropriate responses. He/she will evaluate how well information about problems or challenges, person, and situation was covered. The peer supervisor will also evaluate the practitioner's use of the core interpersonal qualities of warmth, respect, empathy, and genuineness.

11.   The peer supervisor will give one point for each of the contracting skills used by the practitioner.

12.   Continue until each person has been in each role.

Agreement about Goals Evaluation Form

Name of Practitioner_____

Name of Peer Supervisor_____

Directions: Under each category (in italics) is a list of behaviors or skills. Give one point for each specific behavior or skill exhibited by the practitioner. On the scales, circle the number that best represents your evaluation of the appropriateness, effectiveness, or completeness of the practitioner's overall use of the skills or behaviors in the category.

Basic Interpersonal Skills
Communicating Involvement: Give one point for each behavior used by the practitioner. Using the scale, circle the number that represents your evaluation of the effectiveness of the practitioner's overall use of behaviors that communicate involvement.

1.	Open and accessible body posture	_____
2.	Congruent facial expression	_____
3.	Slightly inclined toward the client	_____
4.	Directly face the client	_____
4.	Regular eye contact unless inappropriate	_____
5.	No distracting behavior	_____
6.	Minimal encouragement	_____

1	2	3	4	5
Ineffective				Highly Effective

Observing: The practitioner will describe the client. Give one point for each item described accurately. Using the scale, circle the number that best represents your evaluation of the overall completeness of the practitioner's descriptions.

1.	Facial expression	_____
2.	Eye movement and contact	_____
3.	Body position and movement	_____
4.	Breathing patterns	_____
5.	Muscle tone	_____
6.	Gestures	_____
7.	Skin tone changes	_____

1	2	3	4	5
Incomplete				Complete

Active Listening Skills—Content and Process: Using the scale, circle the number that best represents your evaluation of the accuracy and completeness of the practitioner's summary of what the client said and description of the client's way of speaking including speaking style, vocal tone and volume, and speed of delivery.

1	2	3	4	5
Incomplete				Complete

Beginning Process Skills: Give one point for each topic covered by the practitioner. Using the scale, circle the number that best represents your evaluation of the appropriateness and effectiveness of the practitioner's use of beginning skills.

1. Introduce yourself and your role _____
2. Seek introductions _____
3. Identify where meeting will be held _____
4. Identify how long meeting will last _____
5. Describe the initial purpose of the meeting _____
6. Explain some of the things you will do _____
7. Outline the client's role _____
8. Discuss ethical and agency policies _____
9. Seek feedback from the client _____

1	2	3	4	5
Ineffective &/or Inappropriate				Highly Effective & Appropriate

Exploring Process

Advanced Reflecting Skills: Give one point for each skill used by the practitioner. Using the scale, circle the number that best represents your evaluation of the appropriateness and effectiveness of the practitioner's use of reflecting skills.

1. Reflecting content _____
2. Reflecting feelings _____
3. Reflecting feeling, content, and/or meaning _____
4. Advanced reflecting _____

1	2	3	4	5
Ineffective &/or Inappropriate				Highly Effective & Appropriate

Questioning Skills: Give one point for each skill used by the practitioner. Using the scale, circle the number that best represents your evaluation of the appropriateness and effectiveness of the practitioner's use of questioning skills.

1. Use of open-ended questions _____
2. Use of one question at a time _____
3. Correct use of closed-ended questions _____

1	2	3	4	5
Ineffective &/or Inappropriate				Highly Effective & Appropriate

Person, Problem/Challenge, and Situation Over Time Exploration: Give one point for each item covered. Using the scale, circle the number that best represents your evaluation of the level of clarity and completeness in each of the three areas.

1. <u>Problems or Challenges</u>
   Previous attempts to solve problem(s) _____
   History of the problem(s) _____
   Precipitating factors _____
   Severity or intensity of the problem(s) _____

1	2	3	4	5
No Information				Complete Information

2. <u>Person</u>
   Feelings about having the problem(s) _____
   Effect of the problem(s) on functioning _____
   Personal strengths _____

1	2	3	4	5
No Information				Complete Information

3. <u>Situation</u>
   Effect of the problem(s) on others _____
   Available social support _____
   Demands and stresses in the situation/environment _____
   Strengths in the situation/environment _____

1	2	3	4	5
No Information				Complete Information

Seeking Clarification Give one point for each skill used by the practitioner. Using the scale, circle the number that represents your evaluation of the appropriateness and effectiveness of the practitioner's use of seeking clarification skills.

1. Exploring the meaning of words and body language _____
2. Exploring the basis of conclusions drawn by the client _____
3. Exploring statements that appear contradictory _____
4. Exploring details regarding interaction _____

1	2	3	4	5
Ineffective &/or Inappropriate				Highly Effective & Appropriate

<u>Contracting Process</u>
Skills Related to Reaching Agreement about Problems or Challenges and Goals: Give a point for each skill used by the practitioner.

1. Reaching agreement about problems or challenges _____
2. Reaching agreement about goals _____

<u>Core Interpersonal Qualities</u>
Using the scale, determine the number that best represents your evaluation of the appropriateness and effectiveness of the practitioner's expression of each quality. Write your evaluation number on the line following each quality.

Warmth _____

Respect _____

Empathy _____

Genuineness _____

1	2	3	4	5

Ineffective &/or
Inappropriate

Highly Effective &
Appropriate

<u>Overall Effectiveness of Practitioner Communication</u>
Inappropriate Statements: Minus one point for each inappropriate statement. ____

Total Score: Add each point, each circled number, and the scores on interpersonal qualities to get the total score for the interview.
_____
Score

Written Exercise H: Creating Measurable, Attainable, Positive, and Specific (MAPS) Goals

Objective of Exercise: To practice developing goal statements that meet the MAPS criteria.

Directions: Reread the client examples in Written Exercise G (pages 82 to 89) and create statements that move the process from general goals to Measurable, Attainable, Positive, and Specific goals.

1.   Mother of student

2.   Stepmother of fifteen year old

3.   Overweight client

4.   Client who can't concentrate

5.   Unappreciated client

6.   Think about a problem you have now or have had in the past. Create a goal that meets the MAPS criteria.

Skill-Building 11: Defining Goals and Establishing a Contract

Objective of Exercise: To practice responses leading to defining the goals and establishing a contract. As you know from your own life, you are much more likely to achieve goals that are very clear. If you are working with another person, it is even more important that the goals are clear and that you both understand exactly what you are trying to achieve. Working with clients, you need to take time to help them decide what goals they want to achieve goals. These goals need to be attainable and defined in a measurable, behavioral, positive, specific way so that you and your client will clearly know when the goals have been achieved.

After the goals have been clearly defined, you can go on to establishing a contract for your work together. The contract should identify how often you and your client will meet, how many sessions you will have before evaluating, and any other agreements you have reached related to goal achievement.

Directions for Exercise:

1.   Form groups of three people. You will each play the roles of the practitioner, client, and peer supervisor.

2.   Each practitioner/client session will be fifteen minutes long.

3.   The client will discuss a problem, remembering to stop after every few sentences to allow space for the practitioner to respond.

4.   The practitioner will communicate involvement, listen carefully, observe, start with a beginning statement, ask questions, seek clarification, reflect feelings, content and/or meanings, and reach for agreement about the problem(s) or challenge(s) and goal(s).

5.   The practitioner will also respond in ways to help define the goals, decide when the practitioner and client will evaluate goal achievement, and establish the contract. If you have trouble getting to a defined goal or creating a contract, stop the interview and get the help you need.

6.   During the interview, the peer supervisor will watch the practitioner's use of behaviors that communicate involvement, observe the client, listen to the client, give one point for each item completed on the beginning process list, and keep track of time. In order to evaluate each response, the peer supervisor will write down each response after the beginning statement.

The following activities will be completed after the interview:

7. The client will share how he/she experienced the practitioner.

8. The practitioner will evaluate her/his use of responses that define the goal and establish a contract.

9. The peer supervisor will go over each response and give a point for each type of skill used by the practitioner.

10. The peer supervisor will ask the practitioner to describe what he/she observed in the client and will ask the practitioner to summarize what the client said and describe the process of the client's communication. The peer supervisor will evaluate the practitioner's use of activities that communicate involvement, the practitioner's ability to accurately observe, the practitioner's active listening skills, beginning process skills, reflecting skills, questioning skills, seeking clarification skills, and check for any use of inappropriate responses. He/she will evaluate how will information about the problem(s) or challenge(s), the person(s), and the situation was covered. The peer supervisor will also evaluate the practitioner's use of the core interpersonal qualities of warmth, respect, empathy, and genuineness.

11. With this practice session, the peer supervisor will also evaluate the effectiveness of the practitioner's use of contracting skills. A clear contract is a deal that like any other contract should be written and signed. Just like a contract you might make with say a plumber, your contract with your client should identify the goals and describe the preliminary plans for work such as when you will work together, what fees will be charged, what responsibilities does each person agree to, and when you will evaluate your work together.

Contracting Process Evaluation Scale

Level 1: The practitioner doesn't reach agreement with the client about problems or goals.

Level 2: The practitioner reaches an agreement with the client that includes some understanding of the problems and/or goals.

Level 3: The practitioner reaches an agreement with the client that includes a general understanding of the goals.

Level 4: The practitioner reaches an agreement with the client that includes clearly defined goals.

Level 5: The practitioner reaches an agreement with the client that includes clearly efined goals and establishes a plan for working together.

12. Continue until each person has been in each role.

Defining Goals and Establishing a Contract Evaluation Form

Name of Practitioner_____

Name of Peer Supervisor_____

Directions: Under each category (in italics) is a list of behaviors or skills. Give one point for each specific behavior or skill exhibited by the practitioner. On the scales, circle the number that best represents your evaluation of the appropriateness, effectiveness, or completeness of the practitioner's overall use of the skills or behaviors in the category.

Basic Interpersonal Skills

Communicating Involvement: Give one point for each behavior used by the practitioner. Using the scale, circle the number that represents your evaluation of the effectiveness of the practitioner's overall use of behaviors that communicate involvement.

1. Open and accessible body posture _____
2. Congruent facial expression _____
3. Slightly inclined toward the client _____
4. Directly face the client _____
4. Regular eye contact unless inappropriate _____
5. No distracting behavior _____
6. Minimal encouragement _____

1   2   3   4   5

Ineffective   Highly Effective

Observing: The practitioner will describe the client. Give one point for each item described accurately. Using the scale, circle the number that best represents your evaluation of the overall completeness of the practitioner's descriptions.

1. Facial expression _____
2. Eye movement and contact _____
3. Body position and movement _____
4. Breathing patterns _____
5. Muscle tone _____
6. Gestures _____
7. Skin tone changes _____

1   2   3   4   5

Incomplete   Complete

Active Listening Skills—Content and Process: Using the scale, circle the number that best represents your evaluation of the accuracy and completeness of the practitioner's summary of what the client said and description of the client's way of speaking including speaking style, vocal tone and volume, and speed of delivery.

1	2	3	4	5
Incomplete				Complete

Beginning Process Skills: Give one point for each topic covered by the practitioner. Using the scale, circle the number that best represents your evaluation of the appropriateness and effectiveness of the practitioner's use of beginning skills.

1. Introduce yourself and your role _____
2. Seek introductions _____
3. Identify where meeting will be held _____
4. Identify how long meeting will last _____
5. Describe the initial purpose of the meeting _____
6. Explain some of the things you will do _____
7. Outline the client's role _____
8. Discuss ethical and agency policies _____
9. Seek feedback from the client _____

1	2	3	4	5
Ineffective &/or Inappropriate				Highly Effective & Appropriate

Exploring Process

Advanced Reflecting Skills: Give one point for each skill used by the practitioner. Using the scale, circle the number that best represents your evaluation of the appropriateness and effectiveness of the practitioner's use of reflecting skills.

1. Reflecting content _____
2. Reflecting feelings _____
3. Reflecting feeling, content, and/or meaning _____
4. Advanced reflecting _____

1	2	3	4	5
Ineffective &/or Inappropriate				Highly Effective & Appropriate

Questioning Skills: Give one point for each skill used by the practitioner. Using the scale, circle the number that best represents your evaluation of the appropriateness and effectiveness of the practitioner's use of questioning skills.

1. Use of open-ended questions _____
2. Use of one question at a time _____
3. Correct use of closed-ended questions _____

1	2	3	4	5
Ineffective &/or Inappropriate				Highly Effective & Appropriate

Person, Problem/Challenge, and Situation Over Time Exploration: Give one point for each item covered. Using the scale, circle the number that best represents your evaluation of the level of clarity and completeness in each of the three areas.

1. <u>Problems or Challenges</u>
    Previous attempts to solve problem(s) _____
    History of the problem(s) _____
    Precipitating factors _____
    Severity or intensity of the problem(s) _____

    1_____2_____3_____4_____5
    No Information   Complete Information

2. <u>Person</u>
    Feelings about having the problem(s) _____
    Effect of the problem(s) on functioning _____
    Personal strengths _____

    1_____2_____3_____4_____5
    No Information   Complete Information

3. <u>Situation</u>
    Effect of the problem(s) on others _____
    Available social support _____
    Demands and stresses in the situation/environment _____
    Strengths in the situation/environment _____

    1_____2_____3_____4_____5
    No Information   Complete Information

Seeking Clarification: Give one point for each skill used by the practitioner. Using the scale, circle the number that represents your evaluation of the appropriateness and effectiveness of the practitioner's use of seeking clarification skills.

1. Exploring the meaning of words and body language _____
2. Exploring the basis of conclusions drawn by the client _____
3. Exploring statements that appear contradictory _____
4. Exploring details regarding interaction _____

    1_____2_____3_____4_____5
    Ineffective &/or   Highly Effective &
    Inappropriate   Appropriate

Contracting Process

Skills Related to Reaching Agreement about Problems or Challenges and Goals: Give one point for each skill used by the practitioner. Using the scale, circle the number that best represents your evaluation of the appropriateness and effectiveness of the practitioner's use of contracting skills.

1. Reaching agreement about problem(s) or challenges _____
2. Reaching agreement about goal(s) _____
3. Defining the goal(s) _____
4. Establishing a contract _____

Contracting Process Evaluation Scale

Level 1: The practitioner doesn't reach agreement with the client about problems or goals.

Level 2: The practitioner reaches an agreement with the client that includes some understanding of the problems and/or goals.

Level 3: The practitioner reaches an agreement with the client that includes a general understanding of the goals.

Level 4: The practitioner reaches an agreement with the client that includes clearly defined goals.

Level 5: The practitioner reaches an agreement with the client that includes clearly defined goals and establishes a plan for working together.

1	2	3	4	5
Ineffective &/or Inappropriate				Highly Effective & Appropriate

Core Interpersonal Qualities

Using the scale, determine the number that best represents your evaluation of the appropriateness and effectiveness of the practitioner's expression of each quality. Write your evaluation number on the line following each quality.

Warmth _____

Respect _____

Empathy _____

Genuineness _____

1	2	3	4	5
Ineffective &/or Inappropriate				Highly Effective & Appropriate

Overall Effectiveness of Practitioner Communication

Inappropriate Statements: Minus one point for each inappropriate statement. ____

Total Score: Add each point, each circled number, and the scores on interpersonal qualities to get the total score for the interview.

_____
Score

V

EVALUATING SKILLS

Throughout one's professional life, self-evaluating is an important skill. Self-evaluation allows you to identify strengths, problem areas, and specific points in an interview where you are ineffective or inappropriate. Throughout this program, you have been developing your evaluation skills. In this final unit, you will use all the evaluative skills you have developed to assess your own work. You will also learn to evaluate the effectiveness of your responses.

Determining the Effectiveness of Your Responses

As you develop your skills, you will want to be able to evaluate the effectiveness of each transaction with a client. In this way you can determine more specifically what is effective and what is ineffective. Although evaluating the effectiveness of each transaction is an advanced evaluative skill, it is important for you to understand how to do this type of evaluation so that when you review transcripts of your work you can evaluate the effectiveness of each transaction.

The effectiveness of your statements to clients can be determined by paying attention to the client's response. You may say something that sounds brilliant, but if your client is not ready to hear your statement and becomes defensive, confused, or withdraws than your statement was ineffective. Or maybe you simply use minimal encouragement and your client experiences this as an indication that you are paying attention and continues to explore. Your client's response indicates that your response was effective. If the client moves into further exploration, your response is probably effective. If the client moves away from further exploration, your response is probably ineffective (Hepworth, Rooney, & Larsen, 1997).

Client Responses that Indicate Effectiveness:

1.   Client adds more relevant information about the problems, challenges, or situation.

2.   Client expresses feelings related to the self or the situation.

3.   Client moves to more thoughtful exploration.

4.   Client explores the meanings of the problems in his/her life.

5.   Client agrees with your response.

Client Responses that Indicate Ineffectiveness:

1.   Client disagrees with your response and does not offer correcting information.

2.   Client appears mixed up or confused, does not ask for more information, and moves on. This probably indicates that your client did not understand you. Maybe you forgot and used professional jargon or shorthand, used vocabulary that is not familiar to your client, or expressed yourself in a way that is foreign to someone with your client's ethnic background.

4.   Client continues the discussion but seems more guarded, detached, nonchalant, or mechanical.

5.   Client argues with you. This usually indicates that there is a power struggle between you and your client

6.   Client gives a "yes, but" response. Client responses beginning with a spoken or implied "yes, but" indicates that you have gotten into a rescue position with your client and are offering them advice that they did not ask for.

7.   Client withdraws or becomes more passive. If your client has been becoming increasingly more active in the process and now seems to withdraw or becomes quiet and passive, you probably said something that they were not ready to deal with. Because your timing was off, your response was ineffective. The same thing said later in the process might be effective. The most serious form of withdrawal is to quit working with you prematurely.

Caution   Remember your goal is to continuously improve not to beat yourself up for being less than perfect. Even the most experienced practitioners make ineffective responses regularly. What you want to do is notice ineffective responses, think about what was going on in you that lead you to be ineffective, and figure out how to improve next time around. Fortunately, your clients will not expect you to be perfect. They do, however, deserve practitioners that are continuously thinking about their work, doing self-evaluating, and improving.

Process for Evaluating Videotapes

Now that you have practiced all the basic interviewing skills, you are ready to complete a videotape in which you will use all your skills and do a complete evaluation of your work. In order to give you a chance to show your skills, these tapes should be long enough to allow you to show your skills. Whoever is being your client is playing that role to help you out. If you client is a person who is easily verbal, ask them to be less verbal, to say a few sentences so you will have plenty of opportunities to talk. Real clients tend to be less verbal than your colleagues who are playing the role of client.

After completing your videotape, you will follow the same system for evaluation that you have been doing throughout this course except that in this case you will be the supervisor of your own work. In many cases, your instructor will also review your videotape, written descriptions, transcript, and final evaluation form.

Your first task after completing the videotape is to write out a description of what you observed in your client. This is not an evaluation, it is a description of what you saw. Say things like the client sat very still, her mouth was turned down, and there were tears in her eyes. Note she looked sad and depressed. Sad and depressed are both evaluative words. Make your written observations as complete as possible. Complete the section on evaluation of observing.

After completing your observations, write a summary of what you heard your client say. Again avoid evaluations and interpretations and stick with what you heard. Also describe how the client talked covering speaking style, volume, and speed of delivery. Complete the section of the evaluation on active listening.

Now rewind and play the tape. Fill out the section on beginning process. Give yourself a point for every item that you cover in your beginning statement. Complete the evaluation scale on beginning process skills.

You are now ready to create a transcript of the tape. You will need to write down everything that you said so that you can go back and evaluate each statement. It is okay to write a summary of each of your client statements, but include exactly what you said.

After you have completed the transcript, go back and think about how well you communicated involvement and rate yourself on the final evaluation form.

Read over your transcript paying particular attention to your use of questions. Give yourself a point for each type of question used. Give yourself a point if you only used one question at a time. Complete the Evaluation Scale on use of questions.

Now think over the information you and your client talked about related to the person, problem or challenge, and situation. Complete the evaluation scales related to the person, problem or challenge, and situations. *Remember you are not expected to be able to do everything in this interview.*

Go over your transcript again, name each of your statements as seeking clarification (SC), reflecting content (RC), reflecting feeling (RF), reflecting feeling and content (RFC), advanced reflection (AR), reaching agreement about problems or challenges (AP), reaching agreement about goals (AG), defining goals (DG), or establishing the contract (EC). Give yourself a point for each type of seeking clarification that you used, each type of reflecting used, and each of the contracting responses that you used. Complete the Evaluation Scales on Advanced Reflecting, Seeking Clarification, and Contracting.

Thinking over the whole interview, evaluate your use of the core interpersonal qualities. Complete the Evaluation Scales on Warmth, Respect, Empathy, and Genuineness.

Now go back over your transcript and evaluate each transaction as effective (E), ineffective (I), or inappropriate (IA). Fill in the score for inappropriate responses.

Using the evaluation scale, you will evaluate the effectiveness your responses and give yourself a score on effectiveness.

Effectiveness of Responses Evaluation Scale

Level 1:   The client responds to most transactions from the practitioner by moving away from further exploration.

Level 2:   The client responds to some transactions from the practitioner by moving toward further exploration.

Level 3:   The client responds to about half of the transactions from the practitioner by moving toward further exploration.

Level 4:   The client responds to three quarters of the transactions by moving into further exploration.

Level 5:   The client responds to all or almost all transactions by moving into further exploration.

You will also calculate your overall effectiveness. First, add the scores on all the 16 scales and determine your total number of points on the scales. Then, find that number of points on the scale below. Finally, circle the number above your total number of points.

12	8	4	0	-4	-8	-12
(80-72)	(71-62)	(61-52)	(51-42)	(41-32)	(31-22)	(21-0)

Figure out your total score by adding the points on all the scales and all the individual items. Now congratulate yourself for all that you have learned, recognize all your strengths as an effective practitioner, and decide which of your areas for growth you plan to focus on next.

Final Videotape Evaluation Form

Name of Practitioner _____ Date _____

Directions: Under each category (in italics) is a list of behaviors or skills. Give one point for each specific behavior or skill exhibited by the practitioner. On the scales, circle the number that best represents your evaluation of the appropriateness, effectiveness, or completeness of the practitioner's overall use of the skills or behaviors in the category.

Basic Interpersonal Skills
Communicating Involvement: Give one point for each behavior used by the practitioner. Using the scale, circle the number that represents your evaluation of the effectiveness of the practitioner's overall use of behaviors that communicate involvement.

1.	Open and accessible body posture	_____
2.	Congruent facial expression	_____
3.	Slightly inclined toward the client	_____
4.	Directly face the client	_____
4.	Regular eye contact unless inappropriate	_____
5.	No distracting behavior	_____
6	Minimal encouragement	_____

```
1           2           3           4           5
Ineffective                             Highly Effective
```

Observing: The practitioner will describe the client. Give one point for each item described accurately. Using the scale, circle the number that best represents your evaluation of the overall completeness of the practitioner's descriptions.

1.	Facial expression	_____
2.	Eye movement and contact	_____
3:	Body position and movement	_____
4.	Breathing patterns	_____
5.	Muscle tone	_____
6.	Gestures	_____
7.	Skin tone changes	_____

```
1           2           3           4           5
Incomplete                              Complete
```

Active Listening Skills—Content and Process: Using the scale, circle the number that best represents your evaluation of the accuracy and completeness of the practitioner's summary of what the client said and description of the client's way of speaking including speaking style, vocal tone and volume, and speed of delivery.

```
1           2           3           4           5
Incomplete                              Complete
```

Beginning Process Skills: Give one point for each topic covered by the practitioner. Using the scale, circle the number that best represents your evaluation of the appropriateness and effectiveness of the practitioner's use of beginning skills.

1. Introduce yourself and your role   _____
2. Seek introductions   _____
3. Identify where meeting will be held   _____
4. Identify how long meeting will last   _____
5. Describe the initial purpose of the meeting _____
6. Explain some of the things you will do   _____
7. Outline the client's role   _____
8. Discuss ethical and agency policies   _____
9. Seek feedback from the client   _____

1   2   3   4   5
Ineffective &/or   Highly Effective &
Inappropriate   Appropriate

Exploring Process

Advanced Reflecting Skills: Give one point for each skill used by the practitioner. Using the scale, circle the number that best represents your evaluation of the appropriateness and effectiveness of the practitioner's use of reflecting skills.

1. Reflecting content   _____
2. Reflecting feelings   _____
3. Reflecting feeling, content, and/or meaning _____
4. Advanced reflecting   _____

1   2   3   4   5
Ineffective &/or   Highly Effective &
Inappropriate   Appropriate

Questioning Skills: Give one point for each skill used by the practitioner. Using the scale, circle the number that best represents your evaluation of the appropriateness and effectiveness of the practitioner's use of questioning skills.

1. Use of open-ended questions   _____
2. Use of one question at a time   _____
3. Correct use of closed-ended questions   _____

1   2   3   4   5
Ineffective &/or   Highly Effective &
Inappropriate   Appropriate

Person, Problem/Challenge, and Situation Over Time Exploration: Give one point for each item covered. Using the scale, circle the number that best represents your evaluation of the level of clarity and completeness in each of the three areas.

1. <u>Problems or Challenges</u>
   Previous attempts to solve problem(s)   _____
   History of the problem(s)   _____
   Precipitating factors   _____
   Severity or intensity of the problem(s)   _____

1	2	3	4	5
No Information				Complete Information

2. <u>Person</u>
   Feelings about having the problem(s)   _____
   Effect of the problem(s) on functioning   _____
   Personal strengths   _____

1	2	3	4	5
No Information				Complete Information

3. <u>Situation</u>
   Effect of the problem(s) on others   _____
   Available social support   _____
   Demands and stresses in the situation/environment   _____
   Strengths in the situation/environment   _____

1	2	3	4	5
No Information				Complete Information

Seeking Clarification: Give one point for each skill used by the practitioner. Using the scale, circle the number that represents your evaluation of the appropriateness and effectiveness of the practitioner's use of seeking clarification skills.

1. Exploring the meaning of words and body language   _____
2. Exploring the basis of conclusions drawn by the client   _____
3. Exploring statements that appear contradictory   _____
4. Exploring details regarding interaction   _____

1	2	3	4	5
Ineffective &/or Inappropriate				Highly Effective & Appropriate

<u>Contracting Process</u>

Skills Related to Reaching Agreement about Problems or Challenges and Goals: Give one point for each skill used by the practitioner. Using the scale, circle the number that best represents your evaluation of the appropriateness and effectiveness of the practitioner's use of contracting skills.

1. Reaching agreement about problem(s) or challenges   _____

2. Reaching agreement about goal(s)   _____

3.   Defining the goal(s)   _____

4.   Establishing a contract   _____

1	2	3	4	5

Ineffective &/or   Highly Effective &
Inappropriate   Appropriate

Core Interpersonal Qualities

Using the scale, determine the number that best represents your evaluation of the appropriateness and effectiveness of the practitioner's expression of each quality. Write your evaluation number on the line following each quality.

Warmth   _____
Respect   _____
Empathy   _____
Genuineness   _____

1	2	3	4	5

Ineffective &/or   Highly Effective &
Inappropriate   Appropriate

Overall Effectiveness of Practitioner Communication

Inappropriate Statements: Minus one point for each inappropriate statement. _____

Effectiveness of Responses: Using the scale, circle the number that best represents your evaluation of the effectiveness the practitioner's responses.

1	2	3	4	5

Ineffective   Highly Effective

Overall Effectiveness of Practitioner's Use of Skills and Interpersonal Core Qualities: Add the total score on all of the sixteen scales. The scale below shows the bonus points for overall effectiveness. Circle the number that best represents your total score on all the scales.

12	8	4	0	-4	-8	-12
(80-72)	(71-62)	(61-52)	(51-42)	(41-32)	(31-22)	(21-0)

Total Score: Add each point, each circled number, and the scores on interpersonal qualities to get the total score for the interview.   _____

                                                             Score

APPENDIX A

DESCRIPTION OF EVALUATION SCALES

Communicating Involvement Evaluation Scale

Level 1:   The practitioner communicates involvement very little of the time.
Level 2:   The practitioner communicates involvement some of the time.
Level 3:   The practitioner communicates involvement most of the time.
Level 4:   The practitioner communicates involvement almost all the time.
Level 5:   The practitioner communicates involvement all of the time.

Observing Evaluation Scale

Level 1:   The practitioner is not able to describe any aspects of the client's behavior.
Level 2:   The practitioner's descriptions are minimal.
Level 3:   The practitioner is able to give some description of each of the seven aspects of the client's behavior.
Level 4:   The practitioner is able to give adequate descriptions of each of the seven aspects of the client's behavior.
Level 5:   The practitioner is able to give full and complete descriptions of each of the seven aspects of the client's behavior.

Active Listening: Content and Process Evaluation Scale

Level 1:   The practitioner is not able to give any of the major elements of content of describe the ways the client spoke.
Level 2:   The practitioner is able to minimally summarize some of the major elements of content and minimally able to describe the client's way of speaking.
Level 3:   The practitioner is able to moderately summarize and describe many of the major elements of content and moderately able to describe the client's way of speaking.
Level 4:   The practitioner is able to give a general summary describing most of the major elements of content and a general description of the client's way of speaking.
Level 5:   The practitioner is able to give a complete summary describing the major elements of content and accurately and fully describe the client's way of speaking including: speaking style, vocal tone and volume, and speed of delivery.

Beginning Process Evaluation Scale

Level 1:   The practitioner begins without foundation for the meeting, covering none of the necessary elements.
Level 2:   The practitioner begins with minimal foundation for the meeting, covering two or three of the necessary elements.

Level 3:   The practitioner begins with a moderate foundation for the meeting, covering four or five of the necessary elements.

Level 4:   The practitioner covers all the necessary elements of the foundation for the meeting but appears rote.

Level 5:   The practitioner provides a foundation built on a clear understanding of such things as purpose, roles, and expectations for the meeting and appears focused on the client.

Reflecting Skills Evaluation Scale

Level 1:   The practitioner makes very little attempt to verbalize understanding of feelings, content, and/or meanings.

Level 2:   The practitioner minimally verbalizes understanding of feelings, content, and/or meanings.

Level 3:   The practitioner verbalizes some understanding of feelings, content, and/or meanings.

Level 4:   The practitioner generally verbalizes understanding of feelings, content, and/or meanings.

Level 5:   The practitioner consistently verbalizes understanding of feelings, content, and/or meanings.

Questioning Evaluation Scale

Level 1:   The practitioner uses questions ineffectively and/or inappropriately, uses multiple question, or overuses questions.

Level 2:   The practitioner's appropriate use of questions is minimal, sometimes use multiple questions, and/or occasionally overuses questions.

Level 3:   The practitioner usually uses questions appropriately, does not ask multiple questions, and usually does not overuse questions.

Level 4:   The practitioner's use of questions is mostly effective and appropriate, with no multiple questions and only occasional overuses questions.

Level 5:   The practitioner consistently uses questions effectively and appropriately.

Problems or Challenges Evaluation Scale

Level 1:   Little or no information is discussed about the problem(s).

Level 2:   Minimal information is discussed about one or two aspects of the problem(s).

Level 3:   Three aspects of the problem(s) are discussed adequately but not fully.

Level 4:   All four aspects of the problem(s) are discussed adequately but not fully.

Level 5:   Full and complete information about all four aspects of the problem(s) is discussed.

Person Evaluation Scale

Level 1:   Little or no information is discussed about the person(s).

Level 2:   Minimal information is discussed about one aspects of the person(s).

Level 3:	Two aspects of the person(s) are discussed adequately but not fully.
Level 4:	All three aspects of the person(s) are discussed adequately but not fully.
Level 5:	Full and complete information about three aspects of the person(s) is discussed.

Situation Evaluation Scale

Level 1:	Little or no information is discussed about the situation.
Level 2:	Minimal information is discussed about one or two aspects of the situation.
Level 3:	Three aspects of the situation are discussed adequately but not fully.
Level 4:	All four aspects of the situation are discussed adequately but not fully.
Level 5:	Full and complete information about the four aspects of the situation is discussed.

Seeking Clarification Evaluation Scale

Level 1:	The practitioner does very little to invite understanding of the client's reality.
Level 2:	The practitioner is sometimes able to use questions to invite some understanding of the client's reality.
Level 3:	The practitioner is generally able to use questions to invite some understanding of the client's reality.
Level 4:	The practitioner mostly is able to use questions to invite full understanding of the client's reality, including such things as exploring the meaning of words or gestures, the basis of conclusions, and the process of interactions and apparent contradictions.
Level 5:	The practitioner uses questions to invite full understanding of the client's reality, including such things as exploring the meaning of words or gestures, the basis of conclusions, and the process of interactions nd apparent contradictions.

Advanced Reflecting Skills Evaluation Scale

Level 1:	The practitioner makes very little attempt to verbalize understanding of content, feelings, and meanings.
Level 2:	The practitioner moderately verbalizes understanding of content, feelings, and/or meanings.
Level 3:	The practitioner consistently verbalizes understanding of content and feelings, but not meanings.
Level 4:	The practitioner generally provides reflections that invite the client to a deeper understanding of his/her behaviors, thoughts, feelings, and interactions with others.
Level 5:	The practitioner is appropriately and sensitively able to provide reflections that invite the client to a deeper understanding of her/his behaviors, thoughts, feelings, and interactions with others.

Contracting Process Skills Evaluation Scale

Level 1: The practitioner doesn't reach agreement with the client about problems or goals.

Level 2: The practitioner reaches an agreement with the client that includes some understanding of the problems and/or goals.

Level 3: The practitioner reaches an agreement with the client that includes a general understanding of the goals.

Level 4: The practitioner reaches an agreement with the client that includes clearly defined goals.

Level 5: The practitioner reaches an agreement with the client that includes clearly defined goals and establishes a plan for working together.

Core Interpersonal Qualities Evaluation Scales

Warmth Evaluation Scale

Level 1: The practitioner is cold, detached, and/or mechanical, displaying no concern for the client.

Level 2: The practitioner is generally detached or mechanical, displaying only minimal concern and compassion for the client.

Level 3: The practitioner shows some concern and compassion for the client.

Level 4: The practitioner generally shows concern and compassion for the client.

Level 5: The practitioner communicates verbal and nonverbal expressions of concern and compassion that are appropriately suited to the unique needs of the client

Respect Evaluation Scale

Level 1: The practitioner communicates that the client's feelings and thoughts are not valid or important and/or communicates a belief that the client is not capable.

Level 2: The practitioner communicates that the client's feelings, thoughts, potential, and ability to solve problems are not valid or limited.

Level 3: The practitioner communicates regard for the client's feelings, thoughts, and potential.

Level 4: The practitioner communicates regard for the client's feelings, thoughts, and potential and sometimes invites the client to identify strengths, resources, and capacities that can be used to achieve goals.

Level 5: The practitioner communicates regard for the client's feelings, thoughts, potential, and worth as a person and invites the client to identify strengths, resources, and capacities that can be used to achieve goals.

Empathy Evaluation Scales

Level 1: The practitioner is not listening. She/he communicates no awareness of the client's expressed feelings and expressions.

Level 2: The practitioner occasionally responds to the client's expressed feelings.

Level 3:   The practitioner expresses essentially the same feelings, content, and/or meaning as the client.

Level 4:   The practitioner communicates an understanding and acceptance of the validity of the client's point of view.

Level 5:   The practitioner communicates a clear understanding of the client's felt experience and acceptance of the validity of the client's experience. The practitioner verbalizes previously unexpressed feelings and/or meanings.

Genuineness Evaluation Scale

Level 1:   The practitioner's words are clearly unrelated to his/her present feelings.

Level 2:   His/her words seem to be only slightly related to his/her present feelings. He/she appears sincere some of the time.

Level 3:   The counselor appears moderately sincere but not fully present.

Level 4:   The practitioner generally appears sincere and fully present and sometimes shares his/her reactions with the client.

Level 5:   The practitioner appears completely sincere, fully present and able to appropriately use and share reactions with the client.

Effectiveness of Responses Evaluation Scale

Level 1:   The client responds to most statements from the practitioner by moving away from further exploration.

Level 2:   The client responds to some statements from the practitioner by moving toward further exploration.

Level 3:   The client responds to about half of the statements from the practitioner by moving toward further exploration.

Level 4:   The client responds to three quarters of the statements by moving into further exploration.

Level 5:   The client responds to all or almost all statements by moving into further exploration.

REFERENCES

Bernotavicz, F. (1994). A new paradigm for competency-based training. *Journal of Continuing Social Work Education, 6,* 3–9.

Carkhuff, R. R. & Anthony, W. A. (1979). *The skills of helping: An introduction to counseling skills.* Amherst, MA: Human Resource Development Press.

Cournoyer, B. (1996) *The social work skills workbook.* Pacific Grove, CA: Brooks/Cole.

de Shazer, S. (1985). *Keys to solution in brief therapy.* New York: W. W. Norton.

Egan, G. (1990). *Exercises in helping skills.* Pacific Grove, CA: Brooks/Cole.

Furman, B. & Ahola, T. (1992). *Solution talk: Hosting therapeutic conversations.* New York: W. W. Norton.

Hammond, D., Hepworth, D., & Smith, V. (1977). *Improving therapeutic communication.* San Francisco: Jossey-Bass.

Hepworth, D., Rooney, R., & Larsen, J. (1997). *Direct social work practice: Theory and skills* (5th ed.). Pacific Grove, CA: Brooks/Cole.

Hughes, R. C., & Rycus, J. S. (1989). *Target: Competent staff, competency-based in-service training for child welfare.* Washington, DC: Child Welfare League of America.

Ivey, A. E. (1994). *Intentional interviewing and counseling: Facilitating client development in a multicultural society.* Pacific Grove, CA: Brooks/Cole.

Mahoney, M. J. (1986). The tyranny of techniques. *Counseling and Values, 30,* 169–174.

Meichenbaum, D. & Turk, D. (1987). *Facilitating treatment adherence: A practitioner's guidebook.* New York: Plenum Press.

O'Hanlon, W. H. & Weiner-Davis, M. (1989). *In search of solutions: A new direction in psychotherapy.* New York: W. W. Norton.

Rogers, C. R. (1957). The necessary and sufficient conditions of therapeutic personality change. *Journal of Consulting Psychology, 21,* 95–103.

Rogers, C. R. (1961). *On becoming a person.* Boston: Houghton-Mufflin Co.

Vodde, R. & Gallant, J. P. (1995). Skill training as a place for self-exploration: A qualitative study of teaching social work methods from a Postmodern perspective. *Journal of Teaching in Social Work, 11,* 119–137.

Walter, J. L. & Peller, J. E. (1992). *Becoming solution-focused in brief therapy.* New York: Brunner/Mazel, Inc.

Weick, A. (1993). Reconstructing social work education. *Journal of Teaching in Social Work, 8*(1/2), 11–30.

INDEX

Active listening, 5
    advanced reflecting evaluation form, 58
    agreement about goals evaluation form, 92
    agreement about problems evaluation form, 77
    content and process, 18–19
    content and process evaluation scale, 16–17, 19
    defining goals, 99
    directions for, 15–16
    establishing a contract, 99
    objectives, 15
    questioning evaluation form, 42
    reflecting evaluation form, 36
    seeking clarification evaluation form, 49
    videotape evaluation form, 108
Active listening evaluation form, 18–19
Active listening evaluation scale, 112
Additive empathy, 53
Advanced reflecting evaluation form, 57–61
Advanced reflecting skills, 36
    agreement about goals evaluation form, 92
    agreement about problems evaluation form, 77
    on the communication scale, 63
    defining goals, 99
    directions, 54–55
    establishing a contract, 99
    identifying, 53
    objective, 54
    videotape evaluation form, 109
Advanced reflecting skills evaluation scale, 55, 58–59, 114
Agreement about goals evaluation form, 91–94
Agreement about problems evaluation form, 76–79
Analyzing, 30
Arguing, 30

Basic interpersonal skills, 5–6
    active listening, 15–19
    active listening evaluation form, 18–19
    advanced reflecting evaluation form, 57–58
    agreement about goals evaluation form, 91–92
    agreement about problems evaluation form, 76–77
    beginning behavior, 20–24
    beginning process evaluation form, 23–24
    communicating involvement, 7–9
    in defining goals, 98–99
    in establishing a contract, 98–99
    evaluation scales, 112–113
    observation evaluation form, 13
    observing, 10–12
    questioning evaluation form, 41–42
    reflecting evaluation form, 35–36
    seeking clarification evaluation form, 48–49

    videotape evaluation form, 108–109
Basic interviewing skills, 1–2
Beginning process evaluation form, 23
Beginning process evaluation scale, 21, 24
    description of, 112–113
Beginning process skills, 5–6
    advanced reflecting evaluation form, 58
    agreement about goals evaluation form, 92
    agreement about problems evaluation form, 77
    defining goals, 99
    directions, 20
    establishing a contract, 99
    objectives, 20
    questioning evaluation form, 42
    reflecting evaluation form, 36
    seeking clarification evaluation form, 49
    videotape evaluation form, 109
Beginning statements, 20, 21–22
Behaviors
    that communicate involvement, 7
    focus on, 4
    nonverbal communication, 10–14
Blaming, 30
Body language, 10–14

Clarification; *see* Seeking clarification
Clients
    and basic interpersonal skills, 5–6
    and beginning behavior skills, 5–6
    cultural/gender differences, 25–26
    diversity variables, 25–26
    effectiveness of responses to, 102–104
    expressing understanding to, 25–26
    importance of first impressions, 5
    inappropriate responses to, 30–31
    personal problems or challenges, 71–72
    questioning skills, 38–44
    responses indicating effectiveness, 103
    responses indicating ineffectiveness, 102–104
    seeking clarification from, 45–52
    thoughts *versus* feelings, 27–29
Closed-ended questions, 38
    on the communication scale, 62
Communicating involvement, 5
    active listening evaluation form, 18
    advanced reflecting evaluation form, 57
    agreement about goals evaluation form, 91
    agreement about problems evaluation form, 76
    beginning process evaluation form, 23
    behaviors, 7
    defining goals, 98

directions, 7
establishing a contract, 98
objective, 7
observation evaluation form, 13
questioning evaluation form, 41
reflecting evaluation form, 35
seeking clarification evaluation form, 48
videotape evaluation form, 108
Communicating involvement evaluation form, 9
Communicating involvement evaluation scale, 8, 9
description of, 112
Communication
of inappropriate responses, 30–31
nonverbal, 10–14
poor patterns of, 31
Communication scale
complete, 68
naming responses using, 81–88
naming statements using, 64–65
scoring, 69–71
types of responses, 62–63
Competency-based education, 1
Competent practitioners, 1
Complete communication scale, 68
Consoling, 31
Contracting process
defining goals, 96–101
establishing a contract, 96–101
reaching agreement about goals, 80, 89–94
reaching agreement about problems or challenges, 74–79
steps, 66–67
videotape evaluation form, 110–111
Contracting process evaluation scale, 97, 101
description of, 115
Contracting responses, 69
Core interpersonal qualities, 26
advanced reflecting evaluation form, 60
agreement about goals evaluation form, 94
agreement about problems evaluation form, 79
defining goals/establishing a contract, 101
evaluation scales, 115–116
questioning evaluation form, 44
reflecting evaluation form, 37
respect, 111
seeking clarification form, 51
videotape evaluation form, 111
Cournoyer, B., 66
Cultural differences, 25–26

Defining goals
directions, 96–97
objective, 96
Defining goals evaluation form, 98–101
Diagnosing, 30

Discussing, 2
Diversity variables, 25–26
Doing, 3

Effectiveness of responses evaluation scale, 107
description of, 116
Empathy, 25
additive, 53
core interpersonal quality, 79
practice communicating, 54
versus sympathy, 31
Empathy evaluation scale
advanced reflecting, 55–56, 60–61
advanced reflecting evaluation form, 60–61
agreement about goals evaluation form, 94
defining goals, 101
description of, 115–116
establishing a contract, 101
reaching agreement on problems and challenges, 79
videotape evaluation form, 111
Establishing a contract
directions, 96–97
objective, 96
Establishing a contract evaluation form, 98–101
Ethnicity, 25–26
Evaluating, 3
Evaluation form, 4
Evaluation scales, 112–116
Excusing, 31
Exploring process
advanced reflecting skills, 53–62
agreement about goals evaluation form, 92–93
agreement about problems evaluation form, 77–78
components, 26
defining goals, 99–100
establishing a contract, 99–100
evaluation scales, 113–114
identifying feeling and content statements, 27
inappropriate responses, 30–31
questioning skills, 38–44
reflecting skills, 32–37
seeking clarification, 45–52
videotape evaluation form, 109–110

Feedback
accurate and constructive, 3–4
specific, 4
Feeling and content statements
identifying, 27
writing, 28–29
Final goals, 67
First impressions, 5

Gallows laughter, 31
Gender differences, 25–26

Genuineness evaluation scale
    agreement about goals evaluation form, 94
    agreement about problems evaluation form, 79
    defining goals, 101
    description of, 116
    establishing a contract, 101
    reaching agreement on problems or challenges, 75, 79
    videotape evaluation form, 111
Glib interpretations, 30
Goals
    defining, 96–101
    final versus process, 67
Goal statements
    meeting MAPS criteria, 95
    recognizing, 80

Habitual poor communication patterns, 31
Hostile criticism, 30

Inappropriate responses, 30–31
Interviewing skills
    kinds of, 1–2
    learning methods related to, 2–3
    self-evaluation, 102–104
    videotape evaluation, 105–111

Judging, 30

Labeling behavior, 30
Leading questions, 30

Measurable, attainable, positive, specific (MAPS) goals, 67
    creating, 95
Moralizing, 30
Multiple questions, 38

Naming statements using the communication scale, 64–65
Nonverbal communication, 10–14

Observation evaluation form, 13–14
Observing evaluation scale, 11
    description of, 112
Observing skills, 5
    active listening evaluation form, 18
    advanced reflecting evaluation form, 57
    agreement about goals evaluation form, 91
    agreement about problems evaluation form, 76
    beginning process evaluation form, 23
    defining goals, 98
    directions, 10–11
    establishing a contract, 98
    objective, 10
    questioning evaluation form, 41
    reflecting evaluation form, 35

    seeking clarification evaluation form, 48
    videotape evaluation form, 108
Open-ended questions, 38
    on the communication scale, 62

Peer supervisor role, 3–4
Personal problems or challenges, 71–72
Person evaluation scale
    advanced reflecting evaluation form, 59–60
    agreement about goals evaluation form, 93
    agreement about problems evaluation form, 78
    defining goals, 100
    description of, 113–114
    establishing a contract, 100
    questioning skills, 40, 43–44
    seeking clarification evaluation form, 50
    videotape evaluation form, 109–110
Practitioners
    competent, 1
    evaluating skills, 102–104
    expressing understanding, 25
    inappropriate responses by, 30–31
    overall communication effectiveness, 37
Premature advice, 30
Problems or challenges
    between client and practitioner, 66
    examples, 71–72
    responses that reach agreement about, 73
Problems or challenges evaluation scale
    advanced reflecting evaluation form, 59
    agreement about goals evaluation form, 93
    defining goals, 100
    description of, 113
    establishing a contract, 100
    questioning skills, 40, 43
    seeking clarification evaluation form, 50
    videotape evaluation form, 109–110
Process goals, 67

Questioning evaluation form, 41–44
Questioning evaluation scale, 39–40, 43
    description of, 113
Questioning skills
    advanced reflecting evaluation form, 59
    agreement about goals evaluation form, 92
    agreement about problems evaluation form, 77
    defining goals, 99–100
    directions, 38–39
    establishing a contract, 99–100
    objectives, 38
    person evaluation scale, 40, 43–44
    problems or challenges evaluation scale, 40, 43
    seeking clarification evaluation form, 50
    situation evaluation scale, 40, 44
    videotape evaluation form, 109

Reaching agreement about goals, 66–67
    directions, 89–80
    general form of communication, 67–68
    objective, 89
    responses, 80
Reaching agreement about problems or challenges, 66
    directions, 74–75
    objective, 74
    responses, 73
Reaching agreement about specific goals, 66, 67
Reading, 2
Reassuring, 31
Reflecting content on the communication scale, 62
Reflecting evaluation form, 35–37
Reflecting feeling on the communication scale, 62
Reflecting skills
    directions, 32–33
    objective, 32
    questioning evaluation form, 42
    seeking clarification evaluation form, 49
Reflecting skills evaluation form, 33, 36–37
Reflecting skills evaluation scale, 113
Respect, 79
Respect evaluation scale, 47, 51
    advanced reflecting, 60
    agreement about goals evaluation form, 94
    defining goals, 101
    description of, 115
    establishing a contract, 101
    reaching agreement on problems and challenges, 79
    seeking clarification evaluation form, 47, 51
    videotape evaluation form, 111
Responses
    determining effectiveness of, 102–104
    identifying goals, 89–94
    using the communication scale, 81–88
Rogers, C. R., 26

Seeking clarification
    advanced reflecting evaluation form, 60
    agreement about goals evaluation form, 93
    agreement about problems evaluation form, 78
    on the communication scale, 62
    defining goals, 100
    directions, 45–46
    establishing a contract, 100
    objective, 45

    videotape evaluation form, 110
Seeking clarification evaluation form, 48–52
Seeking clarification evaluation scale, 46, 51
    description of, 114
Self-disclosure, 31
Self-evaluation, 102–104
Sermonizing, 30
Situation evaluation scale
    advanced reflecting evaluation form, 59–60
    agreement about goals evaluation form, 93
    agreement about problems evaluation form, 78
    defining goals, 100
    description of, 114
    establishing a contract, 100
    questioning skills, 40, 44
    seeking clarification evaluation form, 50
    videotape evaluation form, 109–110
Sympathizing, 31

Thoughts *versus* feelings, 27–29
Threatening, 30
Transactions
    evaluating effectiveness of, 102
    naming a series of, 69–71

Verbal communication
    active listening, 15–19
    questioning skills, 38–44
    seeking clarification, 45–52
Videotape evaluation, 105–111
Videotape evaluation form, 108–111
Visualizing, 2–3.

Warmth, 32
Warmth evaluation scale, 33–34, 37
    advanced reflecting evaluation form, 60
    agreement about goals evaluation form, 94
    defining goals, 101
    description of, 115
    establishing a contract, 101
    questioning evaluation form, 44
    reaching agreement on problems or challenges, 79
    reflecting evaluation form, 33–34, 37
    seeking clarification evaluation form, 51
    videotape evaluation form, 111
Writing, 2